Thai home cooking

Thai home cooking

**100 recipes with steps and tips
for easy, authentic Thai food**

Orathay Souksisavanh
Photographs by Akiko Ida

murdoch books

Sydney | London

Foreword

My mother was born and raised in Yaowarat, in Bangkok's Chinatown. My grandfather was a Chinese accountant who left behind his wife and six children after he died from tuberculosis. Having no income, my grandmother would cook small dishes and Chinese snacks that my mother and her sisters would sell after school outside the cinemas.

My mother later met my father, who was from an upper-class Chinese family that had been living in Bangkok for several generations.

My paternal great-grandfather had married a Thai woman who worked in the kitchens of the royal palace in Bangkok. She was the one who prepared family meals and it was alongside her that my mother learnt to cook Thai food.

I grew up in a family where people didn't talk about their feelings and children weren't a part of adult discussions. The only times we could connect and have a proper conversation were when talking about menus for family meals. It was, and still is, our main topic of discussion.

I have long since realised that love in our family is expressed through the dishes we cook. In this book, I am sharing with you all the love I have ever received in my life.

Orathay Souksisavanh

Snacks & starters 12

Salads & dips 44

Curries 84

Soups 116

Stir-fries 144

Meat & seafood 180

Drinks & desserts 214

Resources 244

Snacks & starters

Serves 4 to 6	Preparation 50 minutes	Soaking 5 minutes	Cooking 15 minutes

Miang Kham

Betel leaves with dried shrimp, toasted coconut & chilli filling

**The betel leaves are folded into cones and filled
to make tasty bites, eaten plain or with sauce.**

Filling
40 g (1½ oz) dried shrimp
2 red Asian shallots
40 g (1½ oz) fresh ginger
1 lime
1 pack of betel or piper leaves or
   1 green lettuce (Batavia, Little Gem)
50 g (1¾ oz) unsalted roasted peanuts
40 g (1½ oz) toasted coconut flakes
Green chillies (to taste)

Sauce
1 tablespoon unsalted roasted peanuts
1 tablespoon toasted coconut flakes
15 g (½ oz) dried shrimp
15 g (½ oz) fresh galangal
10 g (¼ oz) fresh ginger
100 g (3½ oz) palm sugar
1 teaspoon fermented shrimp
   paste (optional)
2 tablespoons tamarind concentrate
   (recipe page 255 or store-bought)
2 tablespoons fish sauce
100 ml (scant ½ cup) water

Prepare the filling. Soak the 40 g (1½ oz) dried shrimp in a bowl of warm water for 5 minutes, or until they become plump and slightly soft. Dice the shallots and ginger into small 3 to 4 mm (⅛ inch) cubes.

Peel the lime and remove all the pith, seeds and zest (skin). Cut the flesh into cubes. Remove the white part under the skin and cut the zest into cubes. Set aside in the refrigerator.

Prepare the sauce. Coarsely crush the peanuts, then process them with the coconut to form a fine powder. Set aside in a bowl. In a food processor, blend the 15 g (½ oz) dried shrimp until a stringy powder is obtained. Tip into a saucepan.

Blend the galangal and ginger as finely as possible, then pour into the saucepan. Crush the palm sugar, then add it to the saucepan, along with the shrimp paste (if using), tamarind, fish sauce and water. Cook for 15 minutes over a low heat, stirring regularly. The sugar should be completely dissolved and the sauce slightly caramelised. Off the heat, add the peanut-and-coconut powder. Check the taste. The sauce should be sweet, salty, tangy, in that order. Adjust the seasoning if necessary.

Drain the shrimp for the filling. Clean the betel leaves. Arrange the sauce and all the filling ingredients in bowls. Each guest will make a small wrap by filling a betel leaf and topping it with sauce.

Serves 4 (24 pieces) | Preparation 50 minutes | Soaking 15 minutes | Cooking 25 minutes

Saku Sai Moo

Tapioca dumplings with a pork & peanut filling

These sweet-and-sour dumplings are steamed, then eaten wrapped in a lettuce leaf with herbs.

Filling
2 red Asian shallots
60 g (2¼ oz) salted Chinese radish (Thai preserved radish)
50 g (1¾ oz) roasted peanuts
120 g (4¼ oz) palm sugar
2 tablespoons vegetable oil
150 g (5½ oz) pork mince
½ teaspoon ground white pepper

Fried garlic
6 large garlic cloves
80 ml (⅓ cup) vegetable oil

Tapioca dough
100 g (3½ oz) tapioca balls
300 ml (1¼ cups) water

To serve
1 Batavia or butter lettuce
1 bunch of coriander (cilantro)
Small green or red Thai chillies (to taste)

16 — Snacks & starters

Step-by-step

Prepare the filling. Finely chop the shallots and radish. Coarsely chop the peanuts. Roughly chop the palm sugar. Heat the oil in a frying pan. Fry the shallots and radish for 2 minutes over a medium heat. Add the palm sugar, pork mince and pepper. Cook for 5 to 8 minutes, stirring constantly. Make sure the sugar is dissolved and break up the mince well, then cook until the mixture is caramelised. Off the heat, add the peanuts. Mix together and taste. The salt in the radish is usually enough to season the filling but add a little salt if necessary. Allow the filling to cool completely, then form 10 to 12 g (¼ to ½ oz) balls.

Prepare the fried garlic. Finely chop the garlic cloves. Heat the oil in a small saucepan. Fry the garlic over a medium heat, stirring regularly, until golden, then strain. Store the oil and fried garlic in separate containers.

Soak the tapioca balls in a large volume of cold water for 15 minutes. Drain. Spread out a small amount of tapioca in the palm of your hand. Place a ball of filling in the middle (**1**). Add more tapioca on top and close your hand so as to completely cover the filling with tapioca (**2**). Form a ball using both hands.

Line a steamer basket with a banana leaf or baking paper. Oil the leaf or paper. Arrange the tapioca dumplings in the steamer (**3**) and cook for about 10 to 12 minutes. The dumplings should become translucent.

Use a pastry brush to coat a plate with the garlic-infused oil. Place the tapioca dumplings onto the plate. Sprinkle with the fried garlic (**4**). Enjoy by wrapping the dumpling in a lettuce leaf with coriander and taking a small bite of chilli.

<u>Note</u>
The oil and garlic will keep for several months in the refrigerator. You can use them in other recipes.

Snacks & starters

| Serves 4 | Preparation 40 minutes | Marinating 2 hours or overnight | Cooking 20 minutes |

Gai Tod Hat Yai

Marinated fried chicken wings with sweet chilli sauce

The marinade is named after the city of Hat Yai, in southern Thailand. The recipe was such a hit that it became practically the only, and certainly the most popular, chicken marinade in all of Thailand.

800 g (1 lb 12 oz) chicken wings
1 litre (4 cups) oil for frying
150 g (5½ oz) rice flour

Marinade
5 large garlic cloves
10 coriander (cilantro) stems (without leaves)
1 heaped tablespoon whole white peppercorns
3 tablespoons raw sugar
1 tablespoon ground turmeric
4 tablespoons soy sauce
2 tablespoons fish sauce
50 ml (scant ¼ cup) water

Sweet chilli sauce (home-made or store-bought)
6 garlic cloves
2 red chillies, deseeded
200 g (7 oz) raw sugar
180 ml (¾ cup) white vinegar
1 slightly heaped teaspoon salt
1 tablespoon tapioca starch
80 ml (⅓ cup) water

Topping
3 red Asian shallots
1 tablespoon plain (all-purpose) flour
4 garlic cloves

Prepare the marinade. In a mortar, pound the garlic, roughly chopped coriander stems and peppercorns to form a paste. Then add the sugar, turmeric, soy sauce, fish sauce and water. Use a stick blender to process it all together. If you do not have a mortar and pestle, put everything in a food processor but crush the peppercorns beforehand. Pour the marinade over the chicken and combine. Marinate in the refrigerator for at least 2 hours, ideally overnight.

Make the sweet chilli sauce. In a mortar, pound the garlic and chillies or finely chop with a knife. Put the sugar, vinegar and salt into a saucepan. Bring to a boil. Dissolve the starch in the water, then pour the mixture into the saucepan. Stir and remove from the heat as soon as the sauce thickens. Add the garlic and chilli. Allow to cool before pouring into a jar.

Prepare the topping. Slice the shallots, then coat them with the flour and remove the excess by shaking them in a sieve. Slice the garlic. Heat the frying oil to 180°C (355°F) in a saucepan. Fry the garlic slices, using a skimmer to remove them as soon as they are golden. Then fry the shallots until golden and remove.

Pour the rice flour into a dish. Flour the chicken wings on both sides, then fry in the oil at 180°C (355°F) until they are nicely golden (around 8 minutes).

Sprinkle the chicken with the fried garlic and shallots. Serve with the sweet chilli sauce. You can add chopped coriander leaves to the sauce, if desired.

Note
The sauce will keep for several weeks in the refrigerator.

| Serves 6 | Preparation 30 minutes | Cooking 20 minutes |

Mee Krob

Fried vermicelli noodles with sweet-and-sour sauce

This is like a sweet-and-sour popcorn and is eaten as a pre-dinner snack.

2 red Asian shallots
150 g (5½ oz) palm sugar
90 g (3¼ oz) rice vermicelli
    (e.g. Wai Wai brand)
1 litre (4 cups) oil for frying
2 tablespoons oil
3 tablespoons tamarind concentrate
    (recipe page 255 or store-bought)
2 tablespoons sriracha sauce
3 tablespoons fish sauce
Juice and zest of 1 lime
50 g (1¾ oz) roasted cashews
30 g (1 oz) pepitas (pumpkin seeds)

Finely chop the shallots. Coarsely chop the palm sugar. Break the vermicelli into three pieces.

In a saucepan large enough to allow the vermicelli to expand, heat the frying oil to 230°C (445°F). When the temperature is reached, lower the heat to 180°C (355°C), then fry the vermicelli in small batches for a few seconds. The oil must be hot enough for the vermicelli to expand like popcorn. Set aside in a large dish lined with paper towel.

In a wok or large frying pan, heat 2 tablespoons oil over a medium heat. Fry the shallots. Add the palm sugar, tamarind, sriracha sauce, fish sauce and half the lime juice. Bring the mixture to 115°C (240°F), then reduce the heat to the lowest setting and add the vermicelli (this will allow it to stay crunchy for several days), crushing them a little. Mix together to coat well with the sauce.

Off the heat, add the cashews and pepitas. Serve sprinkled with lime zest.

Tip
Left-over mee krob can be packed into an airtight container and served cut into cubes.

Snacks & starters — 21

| Serves 4 | Preparation 40 minutes | Marinating 2 hours or overnight | Resting 15 minutes | Cooking 15 minutes |

Moo Satay

Marinated pork skewers, peanut sauce & cucumber pickles

500 g (1 lb 2 oz) pork tenderloin
   (or shoulder if cooked on the barbecue)
2 tablespoons vegetable oil

Marinade
100 ml (scant ½ cup) coconut milk
1 tablespoon Madras curry powder
10 g (¼ oz) raw sugar
1 level teaspoon salt

Peanut sauce
2 tablespoons vegetable oil
20–25 g (¾–1 oz) red curry paste (recipe
   page 86 or store-bought)
250 ml (1 cup) coconut milk
100 g (3½ oz) peanut butter
30 g (1 oz) raw sugar
1 level teaspoon salt

Cucumber pickles
1 cucumber
1 tablespoon coarse salt
1 red Asian shallot
1 red chilli
30 g (1 oz) raw sugar
90 ml (generous ⅓ cup) rice vinegar
   or white vinegar

Thinly slice the pork. Prepare the marinade by combining all the ingredients, then pour over the meat and use your hands to mix and evenly distribute the marinade. Set aside in the refrigerator for 2 hours minimum, ideally overnight. After the meat has marinated, cook a small piece in the microwave, taste and adjust the seasoning if necessary.

Prepare the peanut sauce. Heat the oil in a saucepan and fry the curry paste over a low heat for about 3 minutes. Add the remaining ingredients and mix well to obtain a smooth sauce. Bring to a boil. Taste and adjust the seasoning if necessary. The sauce is traditionally sweet, but you can adjust it to your taste. The sauce can be prepared in advance. If it hardens, warm it for a few seconds over a low heat.

Prepare the cucumber pickles. Cut the cucumber in quarters lengthways, then into approximately 1 cm (½ inch) thick pieces. Sprinkle with coarse salt and allow to disgorge for 15 minutes in a colander. Meanwhile, thinly slice the shallot and chilli. Mix the sugar and vinegar together. Pat the cucumber dry without rinsing it and combine all the ingredients. Taste and adjust the seasoning if necessary. Set aside in the refrigerator.

Thread the meat onto bamboo skewers.

To barbecue: cook the skewers for 1 minute on each side over a low heat.
To pan-fry: heat the oil in a frying pan over a high heat and arrange the skewers in the pan without overlapping. Sear the meat for about 3 minutes on each side until browned.
To oven cook: preheat the oven grill and place all the skewers on a non-stick or lightly oiled baking tray. Place under the grill and cook the meat for 4 minutes on each side, depending on the heat of the oven.

Serve warm with peanut sauce and cucumber pickles. For a main meal, serve with white rice.

Serves 4 (16 pieces) | Preparation 45 minutes | Marinating 3 hours or overnight | Cooking 4 minutes

Gai Hor Bai Toey

Pandan leaf marinated chicken

Snacks & starters

Step-by-step

The leaves in this recipe are not eaten. They are used instead to flavour the chicken and to hold the marinade. These bite-sized snacks are normally served with a sauce made from soy sauce, sugar and sesame seeds, but I find they are delicious eaten plain and that the sauce masks the delicate fragrance of the pandan leaves. To my knowledge, this is the only savoury recipe made with pandan leaves.

400 g (14 oz) boneless chicken thighs (2 large thighs)
16 pandan leaves (not too long if possible)
1 litre (4 cups) oil for frying

Marinade
1 slightly heaped tablespoon whole white peppercorns
4 garlic cloves
10 coriander (cilantro) stems (without leaves)
1 level teaspoon sugar
2 scant tablespoons oyster sauce
2 tablespoons soy sauce
1 tablespoon unsweetened condensed milk (optional)

Cut the chicken into approximately 3 × 3 cm (1¼ × 1¼ inch) cubes.

Prepare the marinade. In a mortar, pound the peppercorns, garlic and coriander stems (or crush the garlic, chop the coriander with a knife and crush the peppercorns with a rolling pin). Pour the marinade over the chicken. Add the sugar, oyster sauce, soy sauce and unsweetened condensed milk (if using; it keeps the chicken juicy). Set aside for 3 hours in the refrigerator, ideally overnight.

Clean and dry the pandan leaves.

Fold the leaves. Lay the leaf upside down, hold both ends of the leaf and tie a loose knot, passing the tip of the leaf through the loop (**1**). Turn the leaf over and slide a piece of chicken into the pocket formed (**2**). Grab the tip of the leaf and insert it behind (**3**) to enclose the chicken and make a knot like a tie. Adjust the knot so that the chicken is properly secured. Cut the ends of the leaves.

Heat the frying oil to 170°C (340°F) in a saucepan. Immerse the chicken pandan parcels in the oil and fry for 3 to 4 minutes.

Serve as a snack, as in Thailand, or with rice as a main meal.

Snacks & starters —— 25

| Serves 4 (14–16 pieces) | Preparation 30 minutes | Cooking 6 minutes |

Tod Man Pla

Fish cakes with beans & pickle sauce

Fish cakes
400 g (14 oz) cod fillet
20–25 g (¾–1 oz) red curry paste
  (recipe page 86 or store-bought)
1 egg
1 level teaspoon sugar
2 scant tablespoons fish sauce
10–12 lime leaves
3 snake beans or 80 g (2¾ oz)
  green beans
60 ml (¼ cup) vegetable oil

Pickle sauce
50 g (1¾ oz) sugar
3 tablespoons rice vinegar
¼ teaspoon salt
2 tablespoons fish sauce
½ cucumber
2 red Asian shallots
1–2 red chillies (to taste)

Prepare the fish cakes. Remove the bones from the cod and cut the fillet into pieces. Process the fish with the curry paste, egg, sugar and fish sauce until a sticky dough forms. Take breaks as needed so as not to overheat the food processor.

Remove the central rib from the lime leaves. Layer them in a pile, roll up and chop very finely. Thinly slice the beans. Mix everything with the fish paste and form 14 to 16 small patties using slightly damp hands.

Heat the oil in a large frying pan over a high heat. Cook the fish cakes for about 3 minutes on each side until they are nicely golden.

Prepare the pickle sauce. Combine the sugar, vinegar, salt and fish sauce in a bowl. Cut the cucumber into small cubes and thinly slice the shallots and chillies. Add the cucumber, shallots and chilli to the sauce. Serve with the fish cakes.

Note
Fish cakes can also be served with sweet chilli sauce (see recipe page 18 or store-bought).

Thai beers

The two most famous beers in Thailand are Singha (Boon Rawd Brewery) and Chang (ThaiBev). Both are blond beers.

Singha (pronounced 'singh') means 'lion' in Thai (symbol of royalty and power) and is the country's historic beer. Inspired by a trip to Europe, Phraya Bhirombhakdi, a Thai businessman of Chinese origin, decided to create his own brewery in 1933. The company grew and expanded its range by creating other beers such as Leo (Thailand's third most popular beer).

Chang means 'elephant', an iconic animal in Thailand. It is synonymous with strength, greatness and wisdom. Chang was released much more recently, in 1995. It is the result of a partnership between Carlsberg and ThaiBev, one of the largest beverage producers and distributors in Southeast Asia. It is a popular, cheap beer, often associated with the working class. Some people perceive it as a symbol of social inequality.

| Serves 4 (16 pieces) | Preparation 40 minutes | Cooking 15 minutes |

Kuung Tod

Prawn fritters with rice flakes

Sweet chilli sauce (home-made or store-bought)
3 garlic cloves
1 red chilli, deseeded
100 g (3½ oz) raw sugar
90 ml (generous ⅓ cup) white vinegar
½ slightly heaped teaspoon salt
½ tablespoon tapioca starch
3 tablespoons water

Fritters
½ bunch of coriander (cilantro)
300 g (10½ oz) frozen raw peeled prawns, thawed
1 slightly heaped teaspoon red curry paste (recipe page 86 or store-bought)
1 egg
1 level teaspoon sugar
2 scant tablespoons fish sauce
200 g (7 oz) rice flakes or 125 g (4½ oz) panko breadcrumbs
16 frozen raw peeled prawns with tails, thawed
1 litre (4 cups) vegetable oil

Prepare the sweet chilli sauce. In a mortar, pound the garlic and chilli or finely chop with a knife. Put the sugar, vinegar and salt into a saucepan. Bring to a boil. Dissolve the starch in the water, then pour the mixture into the saucepan. Stir and remove from the heat as soon as the sauce thickens. Add the garlic and chilli. Allow to cool before pouring into a jar.

Prepare the fritters. Roughly chop the coriander. Process the 300 g prawns with the curry paste, egg, sugar, fish sauce and coriander until a sticky dough forms. Take breaks as needed so as not to overheat the food processor.

Prepare a bowl of cold water. Spread the rice flakes or panko breadcrumbs on a small plate. Dip your hands in the bowl of water. Take a little prawn filling and wrap each prawn, leaving the tail exposed, then coat with the rice flakes or panko breadcrumbs.

Heat the oil to 180°C (355°F) in a saucepan. Immerse the fritters in the oil. The flakes must puff up. If they don't, then the oil is not hot enough. Cook for around 2 to 3 minutes. The breading should be golden brown.

Serve hot with sweet chilli sauce.

Makes	Preparation	Cooking
5 eggs	40 minutes	20 minutes

Khai Luuk Kheuy

Breaded & fried stuffed eggs

In Thailand, if a man mistreats his wife, his mother-in-law fries him two eggs served in a tamarind sauce, which is, of course, nice and spicy! In the traditional recipe, the eggs are fried without filling or breading. Here is a reworked version, Scotch-egg style.

5 eggs
1 litre (4 cups) oil for frying

Filling
400 g (14 oz) pork mince (belly, shoulder)
½ onion, chopped
8 sprigs of coriander (cilantro), chopped
1 tablespoon soy sauce
1 level teaspoon sugar
½ teaspoon salt
White pepper (to taste)

Sauce
70 g (2½ oz) palm sugar
4 tablespoons water
4 tablespoons tamarind concentrate
    (recipe page 255 or store-bought)
4 tablespoons fish sauce

Topping
3 red Asian shallots
1 tablespoon plain (all-purpose) flour
Dried chillies (to taste)
3 sprigs of coriander (cilantro)

Breading
2 eggs
50 g (1¾ oz) plain (all-purpose) flour
50 g (1¾ oz) panko breadcrumbs

Combine all the filling ingredients together. Set aside in the refrigerator.

Prepare the sauce. Coarsely chop the palm sugar. Pour the sugar, water and tamarind concentrate into a saucepan. Cook for 5 minutes over a low heat to allow the sugar to dissolve. Remove from the heat and add the fish sauce. Taste and adjust the seasoning if necessary.

Bring a saucepan of water to a boil, immerse the 5 whole eggs and cook for 6½ minutes. At the end of the cooking time, place the eggs into a bowl of iced water, then peel them gently.

Divide the filling into five balls. Spread the ball out in the palm of your hand, place an egg on the filling and gently wrap it with the filling. Then press between your hands to form a ball. Repeat with the remaining four eggs and four balls of filling.

Prepare the topping. Thinly slice the shallots. Coat them with the flour and remove the excess by shaking them in a sieve. Heat the oil to 170°C (340°F) in a saucepan and immerse the shallots in the oil. When they are golden, remove them with a skimmer and set aside. Fry the dried chillies for just 10 seconds.

Prepare the breading. Beat the 2 eggs in a bowl. Tip the flour onto a large plate and the panko breadcrumbs onto another. Roll the balls of filling in the beaten egg, then in the flour and finally in the panko breadcrumbs.

Deep fry the eggs in the hot oil at 170°C (340°F) for about 8 minutes, turning them regularly. Remove and drain on paper towel. Allow the eggs to cool for 5 minutes, then cut them in half.

Place the eggs on a dish. Sprinkle with the fried shallots and coriander leaves. Serve with fried chillies and the sauce on the side, or drizzled on top.

| Makes 20 rolls | Thawing 2 hours | Preparation 45 minutes | Cooking 8 minutes |

Po Pia Tod

Fried pork & prawn or vegetable spring rolls

20 frozen wheat spring roll wrappers (21.5 × 21.5 cm/8½ × 8½ inches)
2 tablespoons plain (all-purpose) flour
1 litre (4 cups) oil for frying

Pork–prawn filling (for 20 rolls)
10 g (¼ oz) dried black mushrooms
200 g (7 oz) water chestnuts (tinned) or taro
230 g (8 oz) onions
150 g (5½ oz) carrots
½ bunch of coriander (cilantro) (optional)
300 g (10½ oz) peeled prawns
500 g (1 lb 2 oz) pork mince
3 teaspoons salt
2 teaspoons sugar
½ teaspoon ground white pepper

Vegetable filling (for 20 rolls)
20 g (¾ oz) dried black mushrooms
60 g (2¼ oz) bean thread vermicelli
230 g (8 oz) onions
200 g (7 oz) carrots
2 large garlic cloves
750 g (1 lb 10 oz) pointed cabbage or white cabbage
100 g (3½ oz) firm tofu (optional)
2 tablespoons oil
3 tablespoons oyster sauce (vegetarian)
3 teaspoons salt
2 teaspoons sugar
½ teaspoon ground white pepper
½ bunch of coriander (cilantro) (optional)

Sides
1 Batavia lettuce (or butter lettuce)
1 small bunch of mint
1 bunch of coriander (cilantro)
Sweet chilli sauce (recipe page 18 or store-bought) or spring roll sauce

Snacks & starters

Step-by-step

Allow the spring roll wrappers to thaw for about 2 hours at room temperature. Rehydrate the mushrooms for 40 minutes in cold water.

Prepare the pork–prawn filling. Cut the water chestnuts or taro into 3 mm (⅛ inch) cubes. Finely chop the onions and grate the carrots. Slice the drained black mushrooms and coriander. Cut the prawns into just under 1 cm (½ inch) pieces. Combine with all the remaining filling ingredients. To check the seasoning, cook a little of the filling in the microwave for 15 seconds, taste and adjust if necessary.

Prepare the vegetable filling. Rehydrate the vermicelli in cold water for 15 minutes, then drain. Chop the onions, grate the carrots and crush the garlic. Chop the cabbage and drained black mushrooms. Crumble the tofu. Cut the vermicelli into four pieces. Heat the oil in a wok over a medium heat and fry the onion, garlic and cabbage for 3 minutes. Add the seasonings and remaining ingredients, except the coriander. Continue cooking for 3 minutes. Taste and adjust the seasoning if necessary. Slice the coriander (if using). Tip the filling into a sieve and allow to cool before finally adding the coriander.

Mix the flour with a little water in a small bowl to form a smooth 'glue'.

Gently separate the wrappers. Set aside under a tea towel to prevent them from drying out. Lay a wrapper on the bench top, tip pointing towards you. Place a heaped tablespoon of filling (about 60 to 80 g/ 2¼ to 2¾ oz) on the wrapper. Fold the bottom tip over the stuffing (**1**), start rolling, then fold in the sides (**2**). Roll into an 8 to 9 cm (3¼ to 3½ inch) long sausage shape.

Brush a little 'glue' on the top corner (**3**) and finish rolling (**4**), making sure to stick the dough well to prevent the roll from opening during cooking. Set aside on a tray.

In a large frying pan or fryer, heat the frying oil to 170°C (340°F). Cook the rolls for about 8 minutes. They should be nicely golden. Drain on absorbent paper and serve with lettuce, mint and coriander leaves. Dip the spring rolls in the sweet chilli sauce and enjoy.

Freezing tip
Raw spring rolls can be frozen. Before frying, allow to defrost for 4 hours at room temperature. They will not be completely thawed, but this will not be a problem. You only need to be careful of the oil splattering when cooking.

Snacks & starters — 35

36 — Snacks & starters

| Makes around 25 pieces | Preparation 1½ hours | Resting 45 minutes | Cooking 15+4 minutes per batch |

Karipap

Chicken curry puffs

The name karipap comes from 'curry puff' in English.

Dough A
300 g (10½ oz) plain (all-purpose) flour
1 small egg, beaten
80–100 ml (⅓–scant ½ cup) warm water
1 tablespoon vegetable oil
½ teaspoon salt

Dough B
150 g (5½ oz) plain (all-purpose) flour
80 g (2¾ oz) softened butter
½ teaspoon salt

Filling
300 g (10½ oz) chicken breast
250 g (9 oz) potatoes
1 carrot (80 g/2¾ oz)
1 large onion
3 large garlic cloves
3 tablespoons vegetable oil
3 tablespoons fish sauce
1 heaped teaspoon sugar
1 heaped tablespoon Madras curry powder
1 heaped teaspoon massaman curry paste (recipe page 86 or store-bought)
1 level teaspoon ground turmeric
½ bunch of coriander (cilantro)
Salt and pepper

Cooking
1 litre (4 cups) oil for frying

Prepare dough A. In a bowl, mix all the ingredients using your hands until a smooth ball forms. Place the dough on the bench top and knead for a good 15 minutes to make it elastic. Divide the dough into two equal portions, cover with plastic wrap and stand for 30 minutes at room temperature.

Prepare dough B. Mix all the ingredients in a bowl using your hands until a smooth ball forms. If the dough is too crumbly, add a little melted butter or

38 —— Snacks & starters

Step-by-step

a little water to make it smooth. Divide the dough into two equal portions, form balls, cover with plastic wrap and stand for 15 minutes with dough A.

On the floured bench top, roll out the first ball of dough A with a rolling pin to form a disc. Wrap a ball of dough B in dough A (**1**) so it is completely covered. Press with a rolling pin and roll out into a rectangle measuring about 30 × 9 cm (12 x 3½ inches), with the short side closest to you. Roll up this rectangle into a tight snail (to form a cylinder). Turn the cylinder a quarter of a turn so that the short side is facing you. Roll out the cylinder (**2**) to form another rectangle and roll it into a cylinder as before. Cover the cylinder with plastic wrap and set aside in the refrigerator while you prepare the filling. Repeat for the remaining portions of dough A and B to form two cylinders in total.

Prepare the filling. Cut the chicken into cubes. Peel the potatoes and carrot and cut into cubes. Thinly slice the onion. Crush the garlic. Heat the vegetable oil in a frying pan over a medium heat. Fry the onion and carrot for 5 minutes. Add the potato, fish sauce, sugar, Madras curry powder, massaman curry paste and turmeric. Season with salt and pepper, pour in 50 ml (scant ¼ cup) water and cook for 10 minutes. Stir occasionally and add a little water if the mixture is too dry. Add the chicken and garlic. Stir and continue cooking for 2 minutes. Taste and adjust the seasoning if necessary. Allow to cool completely, then add the chopped coriander.

Cut slices of dough about 6 mm (¼ inch) thick. You should be able to see the spiral shape in the layers of dough. Roll out each slice into a 9 to 10 cm (3½ to 4 inch) diameter disc (**3**). Place 1 large tablespoon of filling in the middle and close the curry puff, making a half moon shape. Close the edges firmly and pinch with your index finger to seal the curry puff by making a fold (**4**). Repeat the process until all the ingredients are used up. Set aside the completed curry puffs on a tray in the refrigerator.

Heat the oil for frying to 180°C (355°F). Cook the curry puffs for 3 to 4 minutes until golden brown. Remove and drain on paper towel. You can also bake the curry puffs for 20 to 25 minutes in an oven preheated to 200°C (400°F). Enjoy warm.

Tip
The dough and filling can be made the day before and kept in the refrigerator.

Snacks & starters — 39

40 — Snacks & starters

Karipap (recipe page 38)

Khanom tian (recipe page 42)

Makes 25 pieces | Preparation 2 hours | Soaking 4 hours | Cooking 55 minutes

Khanom Tian

Pork & yellow bean rice dumplings

The name of this slightly salty, slightly sweet and peppery cake literally means 'candle cake' because it is only eaten at night during festivals illuminated by candlelight. The leaves in this recipe are not eaten.

1 pack of banana leaves
100 ml (scant ½ cup) oil

Filling
200 g (7 oz) peeled mung beans
3 tablespoons vegetable oil
6 garlic cloves
150 g (5½ oz) pork mince
25 g (1 oz) raw sugar
1 slightly heaped teaspoon salt
1 slightly heaped teaspoon ground white pepper

Dough
400 g (14 oz) glutinous rice flour
1 level teaspoon salt
360 ml (scant 1½ cups) warm water

1

2

3

42 —— Snacks & starters

Step-by-step

Prepare the filling. Soak the mung beans in water for a minimum of 4 hours. Steam them for 30 minutes to cook. Pour them into a container and crush them with the back of a large spoon. Heat the vegetable oil in a large frying pan. Crush the garlic and fry for 2 minutes. Add the pork mince and mix to break up the pieces. Add the sugar, salt and pepper, then tip in the crushed beans. Cook for about 2 minutes, stirring constantly. Remove from the heat and allow to cool, then form 20 g (¾ oz) balls.

Unfold the banana leaves. Cut out 25 rectangles (18.5 × 24 cm/7¼ × 9½ inches) and cut out smaller rectangles (8.5 × 10 cm/3¼ × 4 inches) from the offcuts. Clean the cut leaves under running water and wipe each leaf with a clean sponge. Fold the remaining leaves and place in the freezer.

Gently fold the large rectangles in half. Cut the corners to form an oval when the leaf is unfolded (see page 231). Then place a small rectangle in the middle of each oval (shiny-side down). Brush with oil using a pastry brush. Make a pile of all the banana leaves that are ready and set them aside.

Prepare the dough. Tip the flour into a bowl. Mix the salt and water in a small bowl, then pour gradually into the flour while stirring with your hand. Knead until the dough is soft, stretchy and smooth. Divide the dough into 25 balls of about 30 g (1 oz) each. Lightly oil your hands. Flatten a ball of dough in the palm of your hand. Place a ball of filling in the middle and wrap it completely with the dough (**1**). Repeat the process until all the ingredients are used up.

Fold the bottom of the banana leaf to form a cone (**2–3**). Place a ball of dough inside the cone. Fold the bottom of the leaf over the dough by pressing to form a flat base (**4**). Then fold in the sides (**5**). Close the pyramid by sliding the upper section under the folds (**6**). Repeat the process until all the ingredients are used up.

Steam for 25 minutes to cook. Remove each dumpling from its banana leaf. Enjoy warm or hot.

4

5

6

Snacks & starters — 43

Salads & dips

Cutting papaya & mango

Technique

The quality of a papaya salad is determined by the irregularity of how it is cut. Traditionally a papaya is cut using a knife with a wide and sharp blade, but a slicing knife can also be used. Choose a papaya that is firm to ensure it is fresh and crunchy (from Thailand, Laos or Cambodia). Spanish green papayas are not suitable for this type of cutting because they have a softer, more rubbery texture.

Peel and rinse the papaya. If you are right-handed, hold the papaya in your left hand. Tap it with a sharp knife to make deep incisions (**1**). Slice the papaya from top to bottom. A kind of julienne (**2**) is then obtained. Repeat the process by turning the papaya a quarter of a turn each time. Stop when you see the seeds in the middle and remove the seeds. Papaya scraps can be used in gaeng som soup (recipe page 124) or in vegetable stir-fries.

You can buy a very handy green papaya grater in Asian supermarkets. This grater creates a shredded julienne that is very similar to the result you get by manually cutting the fruit (**3**).

This type of cutting also applies to green mangoes. Choose acidic green mangoes from Southeast Asia, the same as for choosing papaya. This variety of mango is only used in salads or as a snack dipped in a sweet chilli sauce.

Salads & dips

Serves	Preparation
2 to 4	35 minutes

Som Tum

Papaya salad

There are two versions of this salad. Firstly, the version from Bangkok, which is rather sweet and made with peanuts, and secondly, the northern version from close to the border with Laos, which is seasoned with fermented fish sauce. Serve these salads with tender cabbage leaves and pork crackling (kia moo or chicharon).

Som tum thai Thai papaya salad

250 g (9 oz) green papaya
1 carrot
1 ripe tomato
50 g (1¾ oz) green beans or 3 snake
   beans (optional)
3 tablespoons unsalted roasted peanuts

Sauce
2 garlic cloves
1–2 red chillies (to taste)
70 g (2½ oz) palm sugar
1 tablespoon dried shrimp (optional)
Juice of 2 limes
4 tablespoons fish sauce

Grate the papaya and carrot with a knife or using a grater (see page 46). Cut the tomato into quarters. Top and tail the beans and cut into sections.

Prepare the sauce. In a large mortar, pound the garlic and chilli until a paste forms. Add the palm sugar and crush with the pestle. Add the shrimp, pound, then stir using a spoon. Pour in the lime juice and fish sauce. Mix.

Add the papaya, carrot, beans and tomato to the sauce. Pound with one hand and stir using a spoon with the other hand, so that the vegetables are well coated with sauce. Add the peanuts and mix with the pestle. Taste and adjust the seasoning if necessary. The salad should be sweet, salty and sour at the same time.

Som tum pla ra Papaya salad with fermented fish sauce

250 g (9 oz) green papaya
1 carrot
1 ripe tomato

Sauce
2 garlic cloves
1–2 red chillies (to taste)
30 g (1 oz) palm sugar
Juice of 2 limes
2 tablespoons fermented
   fish sauce (padaek)
1 tablespoon fish sauce

Grate the papaya and carrot with a knife or using a grater (see page 46). Cut the tomato into quarters.

Prepare the sauce. In a large mortar, pound the garlic and chilli until a paste forms. Add the palm sugar and crush with the pestle. Pour in the lime juice, fermented fish sauce and fish sauce. Mix.

Add the papaya, carrot and tomato to the sauce. Pound with one hand and stir using a spoon with the other hand, so that the vegetables are well coated with sauce. Taste and adjust the seasoning if necessary. This salad is more on the salty side than som tum Thai, but the sugar and acidity still need to be balanced.

If you don't have a mortar and pestle: combine the palm sugar with the lime juice and fish sauce, then add the finely chopped chilli and garlic. Pour over the vegetables and use your hands to mix, then sprinkle with peanuts and crushed dried shrimp for som tum thai.

| Serves 4 | Preparation 30 minutes | Cooking 8 minutes |

Nam Tok

Lemongrass beef salad

400 g (14 oz) tender beef (fillet or rump)
3 lemongrass stalks
1 red Asian shallot
½ bunch of coriander (cilantro)
½ bunch of mint
1 Little Gem lettuce

Sauce
30 g (1 oz) raw sugar
4 tablespoons fish sauce
1–2 limes
1–2 red chillies (to taste)

Toasted rice (optional)
2 tablespoons raw glutinous rice

Slice the beef into bite-sized pieces. Heat a frying pan without oil, then arrange the beef pieces in the pan. Cook for 2 to 3 minutes on each side over a medium heat. Allow to stand for 15 minutes on a rack while you finish preparing the rest of the dish.

Prepare the sauce. Combine the raw sugar, fish sauce and juice of 1 lime. Then add the chopped chilli.

If you are adding the toasted rice, toast the rice in a dry frying pan over a medium heat until browned. Pound it with a pestle or process to form a coarse powder.

Remove the base and hard outer layers of the lemongrass and finely slice the centre section. Thinly slice the shallot. Pick the leaves from the herbs. When the meat is cold, cut it into thin strips.

Combine the meat, shallot and lemongrass in a mixing bowl. Add 2 tablespoons of rice powder. Pour in the sauce a little at a time, mixing and tasting. Adjust by adding sauce and lime juice if necessary, then add the herbs.

Serve the salad with the lettuce leaves and white rice or glutinous rice on the side.

| Serves 4 | Preparation 20 minutes | Cooking 3 minutes |

Yum Talay

Prawn & scallop salad

3 lemongrass stalks
1 small red onion
4 Batavia or butter lettuce leaves
½ bunch of coriander (cilantro)
½ bunch of mint
300 g (10½ oz) frozen raw peeled prawns, thawed
8 scallops

Sauce

1 tablespoon chilli paste (nam prik pao)
4 tablespoons fish sauce
1 level tablespoon raw sugar
Juice of 1 lemon

Remove the base and hard outer layers of the lemongrass and finely slice the centre section. Thinly slice the onion. Roughly cut the lettuce leaves and pick the leaves from the herbs.

Prepare the sauce. Combine the chilli paste, fish sauce, sugar and half the lemon juice.

Bring a saucepan of water to a boil, immerse the prawns and scallops in the boiling water and cook for 2 to 3 minutes, depending on their size. Drain and put them in a metal mixing bowl. Add the lemongrass and onion. Pour over some of the sauce. Mix, taste and adjust with sauce and lemon juice if necessary. Lastly, add the herbs.

Place the salad in a dish lined with lettuce leaves. Serve with white rice or glutinous rice. You can garnish with sliced chilli, if desired.

Tip

Keep the lemongrass scraps in the freezer as they can be used to make curries or add flavour to a soup.

Variation

You can replace the scallops with squid.

| Serves 2 to 4 | Preparation 20 minutes | Cooking 5 minutes |

Larb Gai

Chicken mince salad with toasted rice

2 tablespoons raw glutinous rice
1 large red Asian shallot
5 sprigs of coriander (cilantro)
3 sprigs of mint
¼ cucumber
300 g (10½ oz) chicken breast mince
1 teaspoon chilli powder (to taste)
3 Batavia or butter lettuce leaves
Salt

Sauce
1 tablespoon raw sugar
Juice of 1 lime
3 tablespoons fish sauce

Toast the rice in a dry frying pan over a medium heat until browned. Pound it with a pestle or process it to get a coarse powder.

Finely slice the shallot. Pick the leaves from the herbs. Cut the cucumber into half moons.

Combine all the sauce ingredients to make the sauce.

Bring 2 tablespoons water to a simmer in a saucepan. Add the chicken and season with salt. Cook for 2 to 3 minutes, stirring well to break up the mince. Tip the cooked chicken into a mixing bowl.

Add the shallot, 2 tablespoons rice powder, the chilli powder and half the sauce. Mix, taste and adjust by adding sauce and more fish sauce if necessary.

Serve with the lettuce and cucumber. The dish can be served with white rice or glutinous rice.

Salads & dips — 55

| Serves 4 | Preparation 30 minutes | Cooking 7 minutes |

Yum Som-O

Pomelo salad

300 g (10½ oz) frozen raw peeled prawns, thawed
2 red Asian shallots
1 tablespoon plain (all-purpose) flour
½ bunch of mint
½ bunch of coriander (cilantro)
100 ml (scant ½ cup) vegetable oil
1 handful of coconut flakes
1 large Chinese pomelo (preferably Thai, but they are more difficult to find)
3 tablespoons unsalted roasted peanuts
Salt

Sauce
80 g (2¾ oz) raw sugar
4 tablespoons fish sauce
Juice of ½ lime

Salt the prawns and set aside in the refrigerator. Slice the shallots. Coat them with flour and remove the excess by shaking them in a sieve. Pick the leaves from the herbs.

Heat the oil in a saucepan and fry the shallots. They should rise to the surface and be golden brown and crispy. Remove from the oil, drain on paper towel and set aside.

Prepare the sauce. Combine the sugar, fish sauce and 2 tablespoons lime juice. Allow the sugar to dissolve.

Toast the coconut flakes in a dry frying pan over a medium heat. When they start to colour, remove from the heat immediately and set aside.

Bring a pot of water to a boil. Cook the prawns for just 2 minutes, drain and allow to cool.

Peel the pomelo completely and remove the central membrane from each quarter. Break the large quarters into two or three pieces.

Combine the pomelo and prawns in a mixing bowl. Pour over some of the sauce. Add the shallots, coconut, peanuts and herbs. Mix, taste and adjust with sauce and lime juice if necessary.

Tip
Strain the cooking oil from the shallots and store in a jar in the refrigerator. It can be used to stir-fry rice or noodles.

| Serves 6 | Preparation 40 minutes | Soaking 20 minutes | Cooking 10 minutes |

Yum Woon Sen

Pork & prawn glass noodle salad

12–18 frozen raw peeled prawns, thawed
200 g (7 oz) bean thread vermicelli
1 small red onion
2 celery sticks
½ bunch of coriander (cilantro)
½ bunch of mint
200 g (7 oz) pork (or chicken) mince
3 tablespoons salted roasted peanuts
Salt

Sauce
90 g (1½ oz) raw sugar
4 tablespoons fish sauce
Juice of 2 limes
1 level teaspoon salt
2 tablespoons sriracha sauce

Salt the prawns and set aside in the refrigerator.

Soak the vermicelli for 15 to 20 minutes in a large container of cold water.

Finely slice the onion and celery. Roughly chop the herbs.

Make the sauce by mixing all the ingredients together in a bowl.

Bring a saucepan of water to a boil, cook the prawns for 1 to 2 minutes, then remove them with a skimmer. Immerse the vermicelli in the boiling water and cook for 3 to 4 minutes, then taste to check they are cooked.

Set aside 2 generous ladlefuls of cooking water, then drain the vermicelli.

Return the cooking water to the pan and add the mince. Cook for 3 to 5 minutes, stirring to break up the pieces. Add 4 tablespoons of sauce and stir.

Combine the vermicelli, meat with the cooking water, prawns, onion and celery in a large bowl. Pour in the sauce gradually so as to adjust the seasoning to your liking. Top with the herbs and peanuts. Serve immediately.

Serves	Preparation	Cooking
2 to 4	15 minutes	45 minutes

Yum Makeua Yao

Eggplant salad

2 eggplants (aubergines)
½ red onion
1 red chilli
5 sprigs of coriander (cilantro)
3 sprigs of mint

Sauce
1 large garlic clove
30 g (1 oz) raw sugar
4 tablespoons fish sauce
Juice of 1 lime

Preheat the oven to 220°C (425°F). Wrap each eggplant in aluminium foil. Bake for 45 minutes. Allow to cool before removing the skin. Drain the flesh in a colander.

Slice the onion and chilli. Pick the leaves from the herbs and chop roughly.

Prepare the sauce. Finely chop the garlic, then combine it with the sugar, fish sauce and half the lime juice.

Combine the eggplant flesh with the onion, chilli and some of the sauce in a large bowl. Taste and adjust by adding sauce and lime juice if necessary. Add the herbs. Serve with rice.

Tip
To make this a more substantial dish, you can add quartered hard-boiled eggs to the salad.

Serves	Preparation	Poaching
2 to 4	35 minutes	30 minutes

Yum Hua Plee

Chicken & banana blossom salad

Banana blossoms do not taste like banana at all. They have a subtle and sweet flavour, like a combination of palm heart, fresh coconut and artichoke.

150 g (5½ oz) chicken breast
Juice of 1 lemon
1 banana blossom
1 red Asian shallot
4 sprigs of mint
6 sprigs of coriander (cilantro)
2 tablespoons toasted coconut flakes
2 tablespoons unsalted roasted peanuts

Sauce
5 tablespoons coconut cream
1 teaspoon chilli paste (nam prik pao)
2 tablespoons tamarind concentrate
   (recipe page 255 or store-bought)
1 heaped teaspoon raw sugar
Juice of ¼ lime

Bring a pot of salted water to a boil. Add the chicken, cover and remove from the heat. Poach for 30 minutes in the residual heat to obtain a soft and juicy chicken breast.

Prepare the sauce. Combine all the ingredients, ensuring that the chilli paste is evenly distributed.

Fill a metal bowl with cold water and lemon juice. Prepare the banana blossom (see page 248): cut the base off the banana blossom and remove the outer leaves if damaged. Chop the heart and immerse immediately in the lemon water to prevent oxidation. This will also separate the leaves from the small bitter banana buds.

Drain the chicken and shred it with your hands. Drain the banana blossom and remove any bud residue. Only the sliced central section should remain.

Finely slice the shallot. Pick the leaves from the herbs.

Combine the chicken and banana blossom in a large bowl. Add some of the sauce, mix, taste and adjust the seasoning if necessary. Add the shallot, herbs, coconut and peanuts. Serve immediately.

Serves	Preparation	Resting	Cooking
2 to 4	20 minutes	15 minutes	10 minutes

Yum Phed

Duck salad

2 tablespoons raw glutinous rice
1 duck breast
1 red Asian shallot
4 sprigs of mint
6 sprigs of coriander (cilantro)

Sauce
30 g (1 oz) raw sugar
2–3 tablespoons fish sauce
1 tablespoon tamarind concentrate
   (recipe page 255 or store-bought)
Juice of ½ lime
1 red chilli

Toast the rice in a dry frying pan over a medium heat. When golden brown, allow to cool, then grind in a coffee grinder or crush in a small mortar. The powder should not be too fine and should still have some texture.

Remove the skin from the duck, cut off a piece of skin and place it in a frying pan over a medium heat so that it releases some fat. Place the breast into the pan and cook for about 4 minutes on each side. Allow to stand for at least 15 minutes on a rack.

Prepare the sauce by combining the raw sugar, fish sauce, tamarind and lime juice. Finely slice the chilli and add it to the sauce (deseeded or not, according to taste).

Slice the shallot. Pick the leaves from the herbs and chop roughly. Thinly slice the duck breast.

Combine the shallot and duck breast in a bowl, add some of the sauce and mix. Add the toasted rice. Taste and adjust the seasoning. Add the herbs just before serving.

Serve with white rice or glutinous rice.

| Serves 4 | Preparation 20 minutes | Cooking 25 minutes |

Sao Nam

Coconut, pineapple & prawn noodle salad

600 g (1 lb 5 oz) rice vermicelli
   (e.g. Wai Wai brand)
400 ml (14 fl oz) tin of coconut milk
16–20 frozen raw peeled prawns, thawed
50 g (1¾ oz) fresh ginger
1 small pineapple
1 lime
2–3 green chillies (to taste)
60 g (2¼ oz) unsalted roasted peanuts
6 sprigs of mint
Salt

Syrup
110 g (3¾ oz) palm sugar
3½ tablespoons fish sauce

Cook the vermicelli according to the pack instructions. Drain and rinse well under cold water. Drain again. Take a small amount of vermicelli, roll into a nest, then squeeze between your hands to remove the water. Repeat with the remaining vermicelli.

Bring the coconut milk to a boil in a saucepan, then allow to cool.

Prepare the syrup. Coarsely chop the palm sugar, then dissolve it in a saucepan with the fish sauce until a thick syrup forms. Allow to cool.

Salt the prawns and set aside in the refrigerator.

Cut the ginger into matchsticks. Cut the pineapple into small even-sized pieces. Cut the lime into quarters. Thinly slice the chillies (deseeded or not, according to taste).

Bring a saucepan of water to a boil and cook the prawns for 1 to 2 minutes. Drain.

Arrange each topping in small bowls or on a large tray. Each guest will take some vermicelli, toppings and mint. They can then season their salad with syrup and coconut milk. Mix everything together before eating.

| Serves 2 | Preparation 5 minutes | Cooking 8 minutes |

Yum Mama

Instant noodle & mince salad

Mama is the most iconic instant noodle brand in Thailand, and without a doubt every Thai person's favourite. Many street stalls offer small, cheap dishes based on these noodles, which are very popular among students and workers.

3 sachets of instant Mama noodles
   (tom yum flavour)
4 sprigs of coriander (cilantro)
1 tablespoon fish sauce
100 g (3½ oz) chicken or pork mince

Sauce
1 tablespoon sugar
1 tablespoon fish sauce
Juice of ½ lime

Prepare the sauce. Combine the sugar, 1 tablespoon fish sauce, lime juice and chilli powder sachets included with the noodles (use quantity to taste).

Cook the instant noodles in a saucepan of boiling water for the time indicated on the pack. Remove the noodles with a skimmer and put them in a metal bowl. Chop the coriander.

Keep 100 ml (scant ½ cup) noodle cooking water in the saucepan. Add 1 tablespoon fish sauce and the mince. Cook over a high heat, stirring vigorously to break up the pieces. As soon as the meat is cooked, add to the noodles. Pour over the sauce, mix together and taste. Adjust the seasoning if necessary.

Add the chopped coriander and divide onto plates.

| Serves 2 | Preparation 10 minutes | Cooking 4 minutes |

Pla Rad Prik

Fried mackerel salad

1 lemongrass stalk
1 red Asian shallot
2 red chillies (optional)
3 sprigs of coriander (cilantro)
2 sprigs of mint
1 teaspoon vegetable oil
1 mackerel (500 g/1 lb 2 oz), cut into
    2 fillets
Salt

Sauce
1 slightly heaped tablespoon raw sugar
2 tablespoons fish sauce
Juice of ½ lime

Combine all the sauce ingredients to make the sauce.

Remove the base and hard outer layers of the lemongrass and finely slice the centre section. Thinly slice the shallot and the chillies (if using). Pick the leaves from the herbs.

Heat the oil in a frying pan over a medium heat. Salt the mackerel fillets, then cook them skin-side down for about 4 minutes. The skin should be golden brown and crispy. Place the fillets on a plate. Add the lemongrass, shallot and chilli. Top with the sauce and sprinkle with herbs.

Variation
The mackerel meat can also be coarsely crumbled and mixed with the sauce, condiments and roughly chopped herbs.

Serves 4 | Preparation
35 minutes

Salmon Larb dip

Raw salmon & lemongrass salad

1 red Asian shallot
15 g (½ oz) fresh galangal
1 lemongrass stalk
3 lime leaves
1 small fennel
3 sprigs of Thai basil
3 sprigs of dill
3 sprigs of coriander (cilantro)
2 sprigs of mint
300 g (10½ oz) skinless salmon fillet

Sauce
Juice of 1–2 limes
1 teaspoon raw sugar
2 tablespoons fish sauce
1 teaspoon shrimp paste (kapi)
    (or 1 tablespoon fish sauce)
2 red chillies (optional)

Prepare the sauce by mixing the juice of 1 lime, the raw sugar, fish sauce, shrimp paste and the thinly sliced chillies (if using).

Finely chop the shallot. Thinly slice the galangal, then cut into matchsticks and finely dice the matchsticks. Remove the base and hard outer layers of the lemongrass and finely slice the centre section. Remove the central rib from the lime leaves, roll the leaves together, then slice them as thinly as possible.

Thinly cut the fennel using a mandolin. Pick the leaves from the herbs and roughly chop some of them. Cut the salmon into 5 mm (¼ inch) cubes.

Combine the salmon, shallot, lemongrass, lime leaves and galangal in a large bowl. Pour over some of the sauce. Mix, taste and adjust the amount of sauce and lime juice if necessary. Add the herbs and mix. Serve with the fennel and with white rice on the side.

| Serves 4 | Preparation 30 minutes | Cooking 10 minutes |

Larb dip

Raw beef & toasted rice salad

2 heaped tablespoons raw glutinous rice or raw jasmine rice
2 lemongrass stalks
2 red Asian shallots
40 g (1½ oz) fresh galangal
4 spring onions
4 sprigs of coriander (cilantro)
3 sprigs of mint
1 witlof
¼ cucumber
300 g (10½ oz) beef for tartare (sirloin, tenderloin or top round)
1 handful of rocket (arugula)

Sauce
Juice of 1–2 limes
1 teaspoon raw sugar
2 tablespoons fish sauce
1½ tablespoons fermented fish sauce (padaek) (or 1 tablespoon fish sauce)
2 red chillies (optional)

Toast the rice in a dry frying pan over a medium heat. When it is golden brown, allow to cool, then grind in a coffee grinder or crush in a small mortar. The powder should not be too fine and should still have some texture.

Remove the base and hard outer layers of the lemongrass and finely slice the centre section. Slice the shallots. Finely dice the galangal. Finely slice the spring onions. Pick the leaves from the herbs and roughly chop. Peel the witlof. Cut the cucumber into rounds.

Prepare the sauce by mixing the juice of 1 lime, the raw sugar, fish sauce, fermented fish sauce and the sliced chillies (if using).

Use a knife to cut the beef into small cubes.

Combine the meat, lemongrass, galangal, shallot, spring onion and 2 tablespoons rice powder in a large bowl. Pour over some of the sauce. Mix, taste and adjust with sauce and lime juice if necessary. Add the herbs.

Arrange the cucumber slices, rocket and witlof leaves next to the meat. Serve with glutinous rice or white rice.

Salads & dips — 77

| Serves 4 | Preparation 40 minutes | Cooking 25 minutes |

Nam Prik Kapi

Shrimp paste dip

½ pointed cabbage or green cabbage
400–500 g (14 oz–1 lb 2 oz) squash
  (kabocha, red kuri, butternut etc.)
100 g (3½ oz) okra or ½ cucumber
200 g (7 oz) water spinach or green beans
400 g (14 oz) mackerel or 500 g (1 lb 2 oz)
  sardines
Oil for frying (optional)
Salt

Dip
35 g (1¼ oz) dried shrimp
3 large garlic cloves
1–2 red Thai chillies (to taste)
30 g (1 oz) raw sugar
45 g (1½ oz) shrimp paste (kapi)
3 tablespoons water
Juice of 2–3 limes
30 g (1 oz) Thai eggplant (aubergine)
  (optional)

Prepare the dip. Process the dried shrimp. Pound the garlic cloves and chilli in a mortar (or process them). Combine the dried shrimp, garlic and chilli with the sugar, shrimp paste, water and juice of 2 limes (to start with). Taste and adjust by adding lime juice if necessary. The sauce should be salty and sour and slightly sweetened by the sugar. Gently crush the Thai eggplant with the flat side of a large knife and mix with the sauce to coat well. Set aside.

Cut the cabbage into quarters and the peeled squash into 1 cm (½ inch) slices. Steam the cabbage, squash and okra together for 10 to 15 minutes. Taste and adjust the seasoning to your taste. Set aside on a large platter. (If you replace the okra with cucumber, cut it into slices and place it raw on the platter.)

Bring water to a boil in a saucepan and blanch the water spinach for 1 to 2 minutes. Drain and place on the platter.

Lightly salt the mackerel and fry them for 6 minutes in hot oil or cook them for 10 minutes under the oven grill, turning halfway through cooking. Place on the platter.

This dish is served like a mezze platter. Each person takes their choice of vegetables and fish, then dips them in the dip. Rice or sticky rice can be served on the side, if desired.

Serves 6 | **Preparation** 25 minutes | **Cooking** 20+25 minutes

Chiang Mai dips

Nam prik ong Pork & tomato dip

5 dried red chillies
2 lemongrass stalks
3 red Asian shallots
6 large garlic cloves
300 g (10½ oz) cherry tomatoes
2 tablespoons fish sauce
25 g (1 oz) shrimp paste (kapi)
2 tablespoons vegetable oil
400 g (14 oz) pork mince
1 heaped teaspoon sugar
100 ml (scant ½ cup) water

Cut the chillies in half lengthways and remove the seeds. Soak for 10 minutes in a bowl of water. Drain the chillies and coarsely chop. Remove the base and hard outer layers of the lemongrass and roughly slice the centre section. Peel the shallots and cut into quarters. Peel the garlic. Cut the cherry tomatoes in half.

In a blender, blitz the chillies, lemongrass, garlic, shallots, fish sauce and shrimp paste until a paste forms. Heat the oil in a saucepan over a medium heat and fry this paste for 3 minutes. Add the pork mince, cherry tomatoes and sugar. Mix well to break up the pieces of meat. Pour in the water and cook for 10 to 15 minutes. Taste and adjust the seasoning if necessary.

Nam prik noom Green chilli & capsicum dip

4 long green chillies
4 large red Asian shallots
1 head garlic
1 large green capsicum (pepper)
2 tablespoons fish sauce
¼ teaspoon salt
1 level teaspoon sugar
Juice of ½ lime
½ bunch of coriander (cilantro)

Preheat the oven to 220°C (425°F). Cut the chillies in half and remove the seeds. Cut the shallots in half and separate the garlic cloves, keeping the skins. Place the chillies, shallots, garlic cloves and capsicum on an oven tray, skin-side up for the chillies. Bake for 10 minutes. As soon as the skin of the chillies blackens, remove the chillies from the oven. Turn over the capsicum, shallots and garlic cloves. Continue cooking for 15 minutes. Remove the shallots as soon as they begin to blacken, then the garlic cloves and finally the capsicum when the skin is charred. Allow to cool before removing the skin and seeds from the capsicum. Extract the garlic pulp. Combine all the ingredients in a mortar or blender. Add the fish sauce, salt, sugar and lime juice. Pound or blend until smooth. Taste and adjust the seasoning if necessary. Chop the coriander and add before serving.

Serve the two dips with crudités of your choice, such as hard-boiled eggs, pork crackling etc.

Salads & dips — 81

| Serves 4 | Preparation 25 minutes | Cooking 30+30 minutes |

Dips we make at home

These dips are often on the menu at family reunions. They are served with an assortment of seasonal vegetables (green beans or blanched cabbage, steamed okra or squash, cucumber, witlof etc.). All this is served together with grilled meats (chicken, sausages, fried wings, crackling) and sticky rice. They're like our version of aioli!

Nam prik makua thet Tomato dip

300 g (10½ oz) tomatoes
4–6 pearl (baby) onions (depending on size)
3 long green chillies
6 large garlic cloves
2 tablespoons fish sauce
1 tablespoon fermented fish sauce (padaek) (optional)
½ bunch of coriander (cilantro)

Preheat the oven to 200°C (400°F).

Cut the tomatoes and the white bulb of the onions into quarters. Slice the green onion stems. Cut the chillies in half lengthways and remove the seeds. Peel the garlic. Place the tomato, onions, chillies and garlic cloves on an oven tray and bake for 20 minutes. Remove the onions, garlic and chillies as soon as they are nicely charred. Cook the tomato for a further 10 minutes or so.

Use a blender to blend the chilli, onion, garlic and fish sauce. Crush the tomato with a fork and remove the skins. Combine the tomato and blended ingredients in a bowl. Add the fermented fish sauce. Taste and adjust the seasoning if necessary. Chop the coriander and add before serving.

Nam prik hed Mushroom dip

300 g (10½ oz) button mushrooms
6 large red Asian shallots
6 large garlic cloves
3 medium pearl (baby) onions
3 long green chillies
3 tablespoons fish sauce

Preheat the oven to 200°C (400°F).

Cut the mushrooms into thick slices. Peel and slice the shallots. Peel the garlic. Cut the white part of the pearl onions into quarters and slice the green part. Cut the chillies in half lengthways and remove the seeds. Place everything (except the fish sauce) on an oven tray and bake for 30 minutes, turning the vegetables regularly. Remove the vegetables from the oven progressively as they begin to char.

Use a blender to blend everything roughly with the fish sauce. Taste and adjust the seasoning if necessary.

Curries

Makes 1 small jar
(about 3 to 4 curries)

Preparation
20 minutes

Curry pastes

Green

2 lemongrass stalks
5 lime leaves
4 long green chillies, deseeded
(or 10 Thai green chillies if you're
feeling brave!)
1 red Asian shallot
4–5 garlic cloves
½ bunch of coriander (cilantro) or
Thai basil
6 g (⅛ oz) toasted coriander seeds
4 g (⅛ oz) toasted cumin seeds
2 g (1/16 oz) whole white peppercorns
10 g (¼ oz) fresh galangal
Zest of 1 makrut lime
½ teaspoon salt
1 teaspoon shrimp paste (kapi)

Remove the base and hard outer layers
of the lemongrass and finely slice the
centre section. Remove the stem and
rib from the lime leaves and slice the
leaves. Roughly chop the deseeded
chillies, shallot, garlic and coriander
(or Thai basil). Pound the coriander
seeds, cumin seeds and peppercorns
in a mortar.

Place all the ingredients in a tall
container and use a stick blender to
make a paste, or pound everything
using a mortar and pestle.

Red

10 dried red chillies, deseeded
2 lemongrass stalks
5 lime leaves
1 long red chilli, deseeded
1 red Asian shallot
4–5 garlic cloves
10 coriander (cilantro) stems
(without leaves)
6 g (⅛ oz) toasted coriander seeds
4 g (⅛ oz) toasted cumin seeds
2 g (1/16 oz) whole white peppercorns
10 g (¼ oz) fresh galangal
Zest of 1 makrut lime
½ teaspoon salt
1 teaspoon shrimp paste (kapi)

Soak the dried chillies in a bowl of cold
water for 30 minutes, then drain well.

Remove the base and hard outer
layers of the lemongrass and finely
slice the centre section. Remove the
stem and rib from the lime leaves and
slice the leaves. Roughly chop the
deseeded long chilli, shallot, garlic and
coriander stems. In a mortar, pound
the drained dried chillies, coriander
seeds, cumin seeds and peppercorns.

Place all the ingredients in a tall
container and use a stick blender to
make a paste, or pound everything
using a mortar and pestle.

Massaman

**Massaman (pronounced 'matsaman')
means 'Muslim'. The origin of this
recipe is said to come from Persian
merchants or from the Malay
influence in southern Thailand.**

5 dried red chillies, deseeded
1 lemongrass stalk
1 red Asian shallot
4–5 garlic cloves
10 coriander (cilantro) stems
(without leaves)
6 g (⅛ oz) toasted coriander seeds
4 g (⅛ oz) toasted cumin seeds
2 g (1/16 oz) whole white peppercorns
5 cloves
6 cardamom pods
5 g (⅛ oz) ground cinnamon
2 g (1/16 oz) ground nutmeg
10 g (¼ oz) fresh galangal
½ teaspoon salt
1 teaspoon shrimp paste (kapi)
Oil (optional)

Soak the dried chillies in a bowl of cold
water for 30 minutes, then drain well.

Remove the base and hard outer layers
of the lemongrass and finely slice the
centre section. Roughly cut the shallot,
garlic and coriander stems. In a mortar,
pound the drained chillies, coriander
seeds, cumin seeds, peppercorns,
cloves and cardamom.

Place all the ingredients in a tall
container and use a stick blender to
make a paste, or pound everything
using a mortar and pestle. Add a little
oil if the mixture is too dry.

<u>Use and storage tip:</u> Once the curry paste is made, set aside the amount necessary for a recipe. Pass the rest
through a sieve, pressing with the back of a spoon to remove excess moisture. Store in a jar in the refrigerator,
with plastic wrap touching the surface or covered with a thin layer of vegetable oil.

| Serves 6 | Preparation 25 minutes | Cooking 30 minutes |

Gaeng Kiew Wan

Green chicken curry with green vegetables

50 g (1¾ oz) fresh galangal
4 lemongrass stalks
2 zucchini (courgettes)
1 large kohlrabi
1 green capsicum (pepper)
250 g (9 oz) snow peas (mange tout)
600 g (1 lb 5 oz) boneless chicken thighs
  (about 3 thighs)
40–50 g (1½–1¾ oz) green curry paste
  (recipe page 86 or store-bought)
4 tablespoons vegetable oil
12 lime leaves
500 ml (2 cups) water
40 g (1½ oz) raw sugar
1 teaspoon salt
6 tablespoons fish sauce
800 ml (3¼ cups) coconut milk
1 small bunch of Thai basil

Cut the galangal into strips. Cut the lemongrass stalks into three sections and bruise them with a rolling pin to release the flavour.

Cut the zucchini into rounds or 1 cm (½ inch) half moons. Peel the kohlrabi, cut it in half and then cut each half into quarters. Remove the stalk, white parts and seeds from the capsicum and cut into strips. Top and tail the snow peas. Cut the chicken into even-sized pieces.

In a Dutch oven, cook the curry paste in the oil over a low heat for 5 minutes. Add the lemongrass, galangal and lime leaves. Pour in the water, bring to a low simmer and allow to infuse for 10 minutes over a low heat.

Add the chicken, kohlrabi, sugar, salt and fish sauce. Continue cooking for 8 minutes. Add the coconut milk and zucchini. Cook for 5 minutes, stirring occasionally. Add the snow peas and capsicum and continue cooking for 2 to 3 minutes. Taste to check the cooking – the vegetables should be slightly crunchy. Adjust the seasoning.

Remove the galangal and lemongrass to make the dish easier to eat. Add the Thai basil leaves before serving. Serve with white rice or rice vermicelli.

Curries — 89

Serves	Preparation	Cooking
3 to 4	15 minutes	5 minutes

Gaeng Khiao Wan Kuung Mamuang

Prawn & mango green curry

This is my favourite recipe when I'm in a hurry and have guests.

500 g (1 lb 2 oz) frozen raw large peeled prawns, thawed
1 large mango (not too ripe)
1 small bunch of Thai basil
1 tablespoon green curry paste (recipe page 86 or store-bought)
500 ml (2 cups) coconut milk
1 teaspoon raw sugar
2–3 tablespoons fish sauce
Zest and juice of 1 lime
Salt

Salt the prawns and set aside in the refrigerator. Cut the mango into even-sized pieces. Pick the leaves from the Thai basil.

In a saucepan or Dutch oven, dissolve the curry paste in the coconut milk with the sugar and 2 tablespoons fish sauce. Bring to a boil, add the prawns and cook for 1 to 2 minutes, depending on size.

Taste and adjust the seasoning by adding more fish sauce if necessary. Off the heat, add the mango pieces.

To serve, sprinkle with the grated lime zest, a drizzle of lime juice and the Thai basil leaves. Serve with white rice.

| Serves 6 | Preparation 15 minutes | Cooking 25 minutes |

Gaeng Ped Moo Nor Mai

Pork & bamboo red curry

300 g (10½ oz) tin bamboo shoots in strips (drained weight)
500 g (1 lb 2 oz) pork tenderloin
40 g (1½ oz) fresh galangal
3 lemongrass stalks
40 g (1½ oz) red curry paste (recipe page 86 or store-bought)
4 tablespoons vegetable oil
350 ml (scant 1½ cups) water
10 lime leaves
1 teaspoon salt
4 tablespoons fish sauce
30 g (1oz) raw sugar
400 ml (14 fl oz) tin of coconut milk

Blanch the bamboo shoots for 5 minutes in a saucepan of boiling water. Drain, rinse with cold water and drain again. This removes the pungent bamboo smell.

Cut the pork tenderloin into very thin slices. Cut the galangal into strips. Cut the lemongrass stalks into three sections and bruise them with a rolling pin to release the flavour.

In a Dutch oven, cook the curry paste in the oil over a low heat for 5 minutes. Pour in the water and bring to a boil. Add the galangal, lemongrass and lime leaves. Infuse for 5 minutes over low heat, then add the salt, fish sauce, sugar and coconut milk. When the curry starts to boil, add the meat and bamboo. Stir and cook for 5 to 8 minutes. Taste and adjust the seasoning if necessary.

Serve with white rice or rice vermicelli.

Serves	Preparation	Cooking
2 to 4	15 minutes	1¾ hours

Gaeng Ped Phed Sapparot

Red duck curry with pineapple

1 lemongrass stalk
2 duck legs (800 g/1 lb 12 oz)
40 g (1½ oz) red curry paste (recipe page 86 or store-bought)
5 lime leaves
200 ml (generous ¾ cup) water
300 ml (1¼ cups) coconut milk
1 tablespoon raw sugar
2 tablespoons fish sauce
½ pineapple
150 g (5½ oz) cherry tomatoes
4 sprigs of Thai basil

Cut the lemongrass stalks into three sections and bruise them with a rolling pin to release the flavour.

Heat a Dutch oven for a few seconds over a medium heat, then place the duck legs skin-side down into the Dutch oven. Cook for 10 to 12 minutes, until the skin is browned. Set aside on a plate, without cleaning the Dutch oven.

Preheat the oven to 180°C (355°F).

In the Dutch oven, sauté the curry paste and lemongrass in the duck fat. Add the lime leaves, pour in the water and the coconut milk. Add the sugar and fish sauce. Return the duck legs to the pan, skin-side up. Bring to a boil, cover and bake for 1 hour 30 minutes.

Cut the pineapple into even-sized pieces and halve the cherry tomatoes. Check that the duck is cooked: the flesh should separate easily with a fork.

Degrease the curry by removing the fat from the surface with a ladle. Add the pineapple and tomatoes. Stir gently and allow to stand for 10 minutes with the oven turned off.

When you are ready to serve, add the Thai basil leaves. Serve with white rice.

| Serves 6 | Preparation 30 minutes | Cooking 15–20 minutes |

Gaeng Pha

Jungle curry

Jungle curry comes from the forest areas of Chiang Mai in northern Thailand. It is one of the few curries made without coconut milk. This is because it is made only of produce collected or hunted in the jungle, and coconut trees do not grow in this region of Thailand. The traditional game is replaced here by chicken.

400 g (14 oz) boneless chicken thighs
   (2 large thighs)
250 g (9 oz) green beans
250 g (9 oz) mini Thai eggplants
   (aubergines)
100 g (3½ oz) Thai pea eggplants
   (aubergines)
200 g (7 oz) fresh baby corn
4 tablespoons vegetable oil
1 tablespoon raw sugar
3 tablespoons fish sauce
5 lime leaves
600 ml (2⅓ cups) basic broth (recipe
   page 118 or good-quality chicken stock)
   or water
4 sprigs of Thai basil (optional)

Curry base
2 lemongrass stalks
70 g (2½ oz) fingerroot (krachai)
40 g (1½ oz) red curry paste
   (recipe page 86 or store-bought)

Prepare the curry base. Remove the bottom and hard outer layers of the lemongrass and finely slice the centre section. Reserve the scraps for cooking the curry. Thinly slice the fingerroot. Pound it all in a mortar and set aside.

Cut the chicken into even-sized pieces. Tail the beans and cut in half. Cut the mini Thai eggplants into quarters. Remove the Thai pea eggplants from their stems. Cut the baby corn in half.

In a Dutch oven, heat the oil and fry the red curry paste, pounded lemongrass and fingerroot for 2 minutes. Add the sugar, fish sauce, lime leaves and chicken. Pour over the broth, add the green beans and cook for 8 minutes. Add the Thai eggplant quarters and continue cooking for 2 minutes. Add the baby corn and Thai pea eggplant and cook for 3 to 5 minutes. The quartered eggplants and green beans should be tender, and the baby corn and pea eggplants should be slightly crunchy. Taste and adjust the seasoning if necessary.

Thai basil leaves can be added before serving. Serve with glutinous rice or white rice.

Serves 6 | Preparation 20 minutes | Cooking 2¾ hours

Gaeng Massaman Nua

Massaman beef curry

Step-by-step

4 red Asian shallots
3 lemongrass stalks
100 g (3½ oz) sweet peanut butter
350 ml (scant 1½ cups) water
6 cloves
10 cardamom pods
1 cinnamon stick
1.2 kg (2 lb 10 oz) chuck steak or gravy beef
6 tablespoons peanut oil
2 heaped tablespoons massaman curry paste (recipe page 86 or store-bought)
3 tablespoons fish sauce
800 g (1 lb 12 oz) potatoes
600 ml (2⅓ cups) coconut milk
50 g (1¾ oz) unsalted roasted peanuts
Salt

Thinly slice the shallots. Cut the lemongrass stalks into three sections and bruise with a rolling pin to release the flavour. In a bowl, dilute the peanut butter by gradually pouring in the water.

Toast the cloves, cardamom and cinnamon stick in a small dry frying pan for 5 minutes over a low heat.

Preheat the oven to 200°C (400°F).

Cut the meat into large pieces and salt generously.

In a large Dutch oven, heat the oil and brown the meat on all sides. Remove the meat without cleaning the Dutch oven. Fry the curry paste (**1**). Add the cloves, cinnamon, cardamom, lemongrass and shallots. Return the meat to the pan, add the fish sauce and water-peanut butter mixture. The water should completely cover the meat. Add more water if necessary. Cover and bake for 1 hour 40 minutes.

Peel the potatoes and cut them into even-sized pieces. Add the coconut milk (**2**) and potatoes to the Dutch oven. Bake again for 40 to 45 minutes. Check the cooking: the potatoes should be soft and you should be able to cut the meat with a spoon. Taste and adjust the seasoning by adding salt and sugar if necessary.

Serve the curry with white rice. Sprinkle with halved roasted peanuts just before serving.

Curries — 99

| Serves 6 | Preparation 30 minutes | Cooking 1¼ hours |

Gaeng Hung Lay

Chiang Mai pork curry

Hung lay curry is named after the Kayan tribe, also known as the Padaung or 'long neck' people, who live in the mountains of the area. The Kayan are an ethnic group that migrated to northern Thailand from neighbouring Myanmar, bringing with them their culture and culinary traditions. This recipe differs from other curries because its ingredients include tamarind and turmeric.

500 g (1 lb 2 oz) pork belly with rind (or shoulder)
2 red Asian shallots
6 garlic cloves
30 g (1 oz) fresh ginger
3 tablespoons coconut oil or vegetable oil
25 g (1 oz) palm sugar
30 g (1 oz) tamarind concentrate (recipe page 255 or store-bought)
2 tablespoons fish sauce
1 tablespoon dark soy sauce
100 ml (scant ½ cup) water
½ bunch of coriander (cilantro)

Hung lay curry paste
5 dried red chillies, deseeded
1 lemongrass stalk
3 slices of fresh galangal
4 garlic cloves
1 heaped teaspoon shrimp paste (kapi)
1 tablespoon ground turmeric

Prepare the curry paste. Rehydrate the dried chillies for 10 minutes in a bowl of water. Remove the base and hard outer layers of the lemongrass. Roughly chop the centre of the lemongrass, the galangal, peeled garlic and drained chillies. Process everything with the shrimp paste until a smooth paste forms. The turmeric will be added during cooking so as not to stain the food processor bowl.

Cut the meat into 1.5 × 2 to 2.5 cm ($\frac{5}{8}$ × $\frac{3}{4}$ to 1 inch) pieces. Slice the shallots and peel the garlic cloves. Cut the ginger into matchsticks.

In a Dutch oven, heat the oil over a medium heat. Fry the shallots. When they start to brown, add the curry paste, turmeric and meat. Sear for 2 minutes, then add the sugar, tamarind, fish sauce, dark soy sauce and water. Cover and allow to simmer for 45 minutes, checking occasionally. Add the whole garlic cloves and half the ginger. Continue cooking for 15 to 20 minutes. The meat should be very tender. Degrease the curry by removing the fat from the surface with a ladle. Off the heat, chop the coriander and add it to the curry, along with the remaining ginger.

Serve with rice.

Serves	Preparation	Cooking
4 to 6	20 minutes	3 hours

Panang Nua

Dry beef curry

1 kg (2 lb 4 oz) beef (chuck steak
 or brisket)
3 lemongrass stalks
4 tablespoons vegetable oil
30 g (1 oz) red curry paste
 (recipe page 86 or store-bought)
15 lime leaves
1 level teaspoon salt
30 g (1 oz) raw sugar
2 tablespoons fish sauce
1.5 litres (6 cups) water
1 small red capsicum (pepper)
400 ml (14 fl oz) tin of coconut milk

Cut the meat into slices about 1 cm (½ inch) thick. Cut the lemongrass stalks into three sections and bruise with a rolling pin to release the flavour.

In a Dutch oven, heat the oil over a medium heat and fry the curry paste for 3 to 5 minutes. Add the meat, lemongrass, 10 lime leaves, salt, sugar and fish sauce. Pour in the water and bring to a boil. Lower the heat, cover and simmer for 2½ hours. (This curry can also be baked in the oven at 200°C/400°F, covered.)

Remove the stalk, white parts and seeds from the capsicum and cut into strips. Remove the central rib from the remaining lime leaves. Form a pile, roll them together and slice them as finely as possible.

Check the cooking of the meat: it should be quite easy to cut using a spoon. Add the coconut milk and cook for a further 30 minutes over a low heat. Then add the capsicum and stir. Taste and adjust the seasoning if necessary. Sprinkle with finely chopped lime leaves before serving the curry with white rice.

| Serves 4 | Preparation 10 minutes | Cooking 25 minutes |

Choo Chee Pla

Red fish curry

Choo chee curry comes from southern Thailand and is usually made with seafood. Fish can be replaced by prawns or squid, or a combination can be used. It's important not to overcook the ingredients.

6–8 lime leaves
500 g (1 lb 2 oz) monkfish or other firm fish (pollock, grouper, hake)
2 tablespoons coconut oil or vegetable oil
25–40 g (1–1½ oz) red curry paste (recipe page 86 or store-bought)
250 ml (1 cup) coconut cream
1 level tablespoon raw sugar
1 tablespoon fish sauce

Remove the central rib from the lime leaves. Form a pile, roll them up and slice as finely as possible. Cut the fish into even-sized pieces.

Heat the oil in a saucepan or large frying pan over a medium heat. Fry the curry paste for 3 minutes. Add the coconut cream, sugar, fish sauce and half the lime leaves. Reduce for 10 minutes over a medium heat. Add the fish and cook for an additional 10 minutes, stirring occasionally. Taste and adjust by adding fish sauce if necessary.

Sprinkle over the remaining lime leaves. Serve with rice.

| Serves 6 | Preparation 25 minutes | Cooking 20 minutes |

Gaeng Na Nao

Winter vegetable curry

300 g (10½ oz) squash (kabocha, red kuri, butternut etc.)
300 g (10½ oz) sweet potato
300 g (10½ oz) choko (chayote) or kohlrabi
300 g (10½ oz) flat green beans (Romano beans)
150 g (5½ oz) shimeji mushrooms or button mushrooms
150 g (5½ oz) firm tofu or tempeh
3 tablespoons coconut oil or vegetable oil
2 heaped tablespoons massaman curry paste (recipe page 86 or store-bought)
300 ml (1¼ cups) water
80 g (2¾ oz) unsweetened smooth peanut butter
1 slightly heaped tablespoon raw sugar
2 level teaspoons salt
500 ml (2 cups) coconut milk
Zest and juice of 1 lime (optional)

Cut the squash, sweet potato and choko into even-sized pieces. Cut the flat beans into thirds, then into strips. Separate the shimeji mushrooms or cut the button mushrooms into 4 to 6 pieces, depending on their size. Cut the tofu into even-sized pieces.

In a large Dutch oven, heat the oil over a medium heat. Fry the curry paste for 3 minutes. Pour in the water and dissolve the peanut butter. Add the sugar, salt, coconut milk and pieces of squash, sweet potato and choko. Cover and cook for 10 minutes. Add the tofu and flat beans and cook for 4 minutes, uncovered. Add the mushrooms and cook for 2 minutes, occasionally stirring gently. Taste and adjust the seasoning if necessary.

Serve with your choice of rice. Add some lime zest and a drizzle of lime juice when serving, if desired.

Curries — 109

| Serves 4 to 6 | Preparation 15 minutes | Cooking 25 minutes |

Gaeng Na Ron

Summer vegetable curry

2 small eggplants (aubergines)
2 medium zucchini (courgettes)
1 red capsicum (pepper)
3 tablespoons coconut oil or vegetable oil
1–2 tablespoons green curry paste
   (recipe page 86 or store-bought)
250 ml (1 cup) water
80 g (2¾ oz) soy protein
1 slightly heaped tablespoon raw sugar
2 tablespoons fish sauce or 1 heaped
   teaspoon salt
500 ml (2 cups) coconut milk
1 bunch of Thai basil

Cut the eggplants and zucchini into even-sized pieces, without peeling. Remove the stalk, white parts and seeds from the capsicum and cut into strips.

In a Dutch oven, heat the oil over a medium heat. Fry the curry paste for 3 minutes. Pour in the water, add the soy protein, sugar and fish sauce (or salt). Cook for 8 to 10 minutes. Pour in the coconut milk, add the eggplant and cook for 5 minutes. Add the zucchini and continue cooking for 3 minutes. Then add the capsicum and cook for 2 minutes. Taste and adjust the seasoning and cooking time if necessary. Remove from the heat and stir in the Thai basil leaves.

Serve with rice or rice vermicelli.

Serves 4 | Soaking 4 hours or overnight | Cooking 30 minutes

Khao Niaow

Sticky rice

Technique

1

2

In Thailand and Laos, glutinous rice is cooked in a conical bamboo basket (huad) that is placed on a special aluminium (1) or terracotta pan. The basket is covered with a lid and then the rice is turned over in a single flip halfway through cooking. Once the rice is cooked, it is stored in another bamboo basket with a lid (kratip khao). The basket keeps the rice warm and allows good air circulation, which prevents the rice from becoming too moist and losing the texture of the grains.

Traditionally, you use your hands to form a rice ball that is then dipped in a sauce (nam prik) or served alongside various dishes.

The conical shape of the huad allows steam to rise through the gaps in the basket, enveloping the grains of rice and ensuring even cooking. The cone also allows you to cook a large quantity of rice, while making it easy to remove from the mould.

Soak 500 g (1 lb 2 oz) glutinous rice for a minimum of 4 hours (ideally overnight) in a large container of cold water.

Drain the rice. In a steamer, bring water to a boil. Line the basket with a thin damp tea towel. Tip in the rice (2) and cook for 30 minutes, turning it halfway through cooking with a spatula.

To keep the rice warm and avoid a crust forming, keep it in a bamboo basket or covered with a tea towel.

Serves 4 | Cooking 10–15 minutes | Standing 15 minutes

Khao San

Thai rice

Technique

3 volumes of rice (160 ml/5¼ fl oz cup supplied with the rice cooker or 413 g/14½ oz rice)
3 volumes of water (500 ml/2 cups water)

Rinse the rice twice, rubbing it between your hands to remove excess starch and any impurities.

Rice cooker
Tip the rice into the rice cooker bowl. Add water and switch on to start cooking.

Saucepan
In a thick-bottomed saucepan, bring the rice and water to a boil over a medium heat. Cook for 2 minutes, covered, then lower the heat and continue cooking for 10 to 15 minutes over a low heat until the water has evaporated. Remove from the heat and stand for 15 minutes without opening the lid.

Curries — 115

Soups

| Makes 1.5–2 litres (6–8 cups) broth | Preparation 10 minutes | Cooking 1–2 hours |

Basic broth

Chicken and/or pork bone broth

2 onions
2 celery stalks
2 carrots
1.5 kg (3 lb 5 oz) chicken and/or pork bones or 1 whole chicken
1 teaspoon salt
3 litres (12 cups) water

Cut the onions in half, the celery in thirds and the carrots into large sections.

Place the bones or whole chicken into a large pot with the vegetables and the salt. Pour in the water and bring to a boil. Skim, lower the heat and simmer for 1 hour for bones or 2 hours for a whole chicken. Strain, allow to cool, then degrease by removing the fat from the surface using a ladle.

Use the broth in soup recipes, noodle soups or sukiyaki (recipe page 140).

To eat the chicken, shred the meat, then use it to spice up various recipes such as noodles, fried rice or salads.

Soups — 119

| Serves 4 | Preparation 20 minutes | Cooking 25 minutes |

Tom Yum Kuung

Prawn & lemongrass soup

200 g (7 oz) oyster mushrooms or
button mushrooms
3 lemongrass stalks
40 g (1½ oz) fresh galangal
1–2 red chillies (to taste)
2 tomatoes
1.5 litres (6 cups) basic broth
(recipe page 118)
12 lime leaves
4–5 tablespoons fish sauce
1 tablespoon chilli paste
(nam prik pao)
8–12 frozen large king prawns, thawed
100 g (3½ oz) fresh baby corn (optional)
Juice of 1–2 limes
3 spring onion stems
½ bunch of coriander (cilantro)

Clean the mushrooms and roughly tear the larger ones into pieces. Cut the lemongrass stalks into three sections and bruise them with a rolling pin to release the flavour. Cut the galangal into strips. Slice the chillies. Cut the tomatoes into quarters.

Pour the broth into a saucepan, add the lime leaves, lemongrass and galangal. Bring to a low simmer and allow to infuse for 15 minutes over a low heat. Add the fish sauce, chilli paste, sliced chilli, tomato quarters, prawns and mushrooms. Increase the heat and cook for 5 minutes. Add the baby corn (if using) and continue cooking for 2 minutes.

Off the heat, pour in half the lime juice first, taste and adjust the seasoning if necessary. The soup should be sour, salty and slightly sweet, as well as spicy if you like it hot!

When ready to serve, slice the spring onion and chop the coriander before adding to the soup.

Broth tip
If you haven't had time to prepare the basic broth, add 2 sliced chicken breasts at the same time as the prawns. Adjust the seasoning.

Serves 6 | Preparation 15 minutes | Cooking 20 minutes

Tom Kha Gai

Coconut, galangal, chicken & mushroom soup

600 g (1 lb 5 oz) chicken breast or boneless chicken thighs
500 g (1 lb 2 oz) button mushrooms or oyster mushrooms, or a combination of both
2 red chillies (optional)
60 g (2¼ oz) fresh galangal
4 lemongrass stalks
800 ml (3¼ cups) water
10 lime leaves
40 g (1½ oz) palm sugar
1 level teaspoon salt
6 tablespoons fish sauce
600 ml (2⅓ cups) coconut milk
Juice of 2 limes
6 sprigs of coriander (cilantro)

Slice the chicken. Clean the mushrooms and cut them into quarters or into six depending on their size. Slice the chillies (if using).

Cut the galangal into strips. Cut the lemongrass stalks into three sections and bruise them with a rolling pin to release the flavour.

Pour the water into a saucepan, add the lemongrass, galangal and lime leaves. Bring to a boil, then lower the heat and allow to infuse over a low simmer for 10 minutes. Add the palm sugar, salt, fish sauce and sliced chilli. Mix together. Once the sugar has dissolved, pour in the coconut milk. Bring to simmer again, then add the chicken and mushrooms. Cook for a further 5 to 6 minutes over a medium heat.

Off the heat, add the juice of 1 lime. Remove the galangal, lemongrass and lime leaves, which are not eaten.

Serve with the coriander, roughly chopped, if desired. Guests will adjust the seasoning in their bowl by adding a drizzle of lime juice or a little fish sauce.

Serves	Preparation	Cooking
4 to 6	30 minutes	20 minutes

Gaeng Som

Sour tamarind fish soup & water spinach

350 g (12 oz) daikon
300 g (10½ oz) Chinese cabbage
250 g (9 oz) water spinach
1 litre (4 cups) basic broth (recipe page 118)
400 g (14 oz) cod or pollock, steaks or pieces
3 tablespoons tamarind concentrate (recipe page 255 or store-bought)
30 g (1 oz) palm sugar
2 tablespoons fish sauce
½ lime

Spicy paste
5 dried red chillies, deseeded
1 red Asian shallot
45 g (1½ oz) fingerroot (krachai)
3 garlic cloves
1 slightly heaped teaspoon shrimp paste (kapi)

Prepare the spicy paste. Rehydrate the dried chillies for 10 minutes in a bowl of water and drain without discarding the water. Coarsely chop the shallot and slice the fingerroot. Process the chillies, shallot, fingerroot, garlic and shrimp paste until a smooth paste forms. Add a little of the chilli soaking water to help make the paste.

Cut the daikon and Chinese cabbage into even-sized pieces. Cut the water spinach into three or four sections.

In a large Dutch oven, heat the broth over a medium heat. Take 80 g (2¾ oz) fish and cook for 20 seconds in the broth. Pound the fish with a pestle to form a paste. Pour this paste into the broth with the spicy paste. Add the daikon, tamarind, sugar and fish sauce. Cook for 12 minutes. Add the remaining fish, along with the Chinese cabbage and water spinach. Cook for a further 3 to 5 minutes. Taste and adjust the seasoning if necessary.

Serve with a squeeze of lime juice. The soup can be eaten as a starter or as a main with rice.

Soups — 125

| Serves 6 | Preparation 25 minutes | Cooking 15 minutes |

Gaeng Liang

Vegetable & prawn soup

300 g (10½ oz) squash (kabocha, red kuri, butternut etc.)
300 g (10½ oz) choko (chayote)
150 g (5½ oz) oyster mushrooms
100 g (3½ oz) fresh baby corn (optional)
1 litre (4 cups) basic broth (recipe page 118)
2–3 tablespoons fish sauce
400 g (14 oz) raw peeled prawns (or sliced chicken)
1 bunch of Thai basil

Spicy paste
1 large red Asian shallot
30 g (1 oz) fingerroot (krachai)
25 g (1 oz) dried prawns
1 scant teaspoon shrimp paste (kapi)
½ teaspoon ground white pepper

Cut the squash and choko into even-sized pieces, about the same size. Tear the largest oyster mushrooms into pieces. Cut the baby corn (if using) in half or thirds.

Prepare the spicy paste. Coarsely chop the shallot and slice the fingerroot. Process the dried prawns until a stringy powder is obtained. Add the shallot, fingerroot, shrimp paste and pepper. Process until a smooth paste forms. Add a little water if necessary.

Add the spicy paste, broth and 2 tablespoons fish sauce to a large saucepan. Bring to a boil. Add the choko pieces and cook for 3 minutes. Add the squash and cook for 6 minutes. Add the oyster mushrooms, corn and prawns, then cook for about 3 minutes. Taste and adjust the seasoning. Add the Thai basil leaves just before serving.

Broth tip
If you haven't had time to prepare the basic broth, add 1 litre (4 cups) water and 2 sliced chicken breasts at the same time as the squash. Adjust the seasoning.

| Serves 4 | Preparation 40 minutes | Soaking 40 minutes | Cooking 10 minutes |

Yen Ta Fo

Pink noodle soup with seafood

Yen ta fo soup is famous for its unique pink-red colour, which comes from fermented red tofu (a Chinese condiment). It was created in the 1950s and is a very popular dish in Bangkok. It is mostly prepared with seafood, such as fish balls, prawns and squid.

250 g (9 oz) rice vermicelli
  (e.g. Wai Wai brand)
200 g (7 oz) water spinach
6 cubes of fried tofu (optional)
200 g (7 oz) squid fillets
12 frozen raw peeled prawns, thawed

Fried garlic
6 large garlic cloves
80 ml (⅓ cup) vegetable oil

Yen ta fo sauce
70 g (2½ oz) fermented red tofu cubes
2 tablespoons fish sauce
2 tablespoons ketchup
3 tablespoons sriracha sauce
6 tablespoons white vinegar
40 g (1½ oz) raw sugar
1 garlic clove, crushed

Broth
1 litre (4 cups) basic broth (recipe
  page 118)
1 teaspoon raw sugar
½ teaspoon salt

Soak the vermicelli in a large volume of cold water for 40 minutes.

Prepare the fried garlic. Finely chop the garlic cloves. Heat the oil in a small saucepan over a medium heat and fry the garlic, stirring regularly. As soon as it begins to colour, turn off the heat. The garlic will continue to cook in the hot oil. Strain. Store the oil and fried garlic in separate containers.

Combine all the sauce ingredients to make the yen ta fo sauce.

Cut the water spinach into three or four sections. Cut the fried tofu cubes (if using) in half. Score the squid, then cut them into 1.5 cm (⅝ inch) wide strips.

Bring a large saucepan of water to a boil and cook the drained vermicelli according to the pack instructions. Drain and divide into four bowls.

Bring the broth to a boil in a large saucepan with the sugar and salt. Add the fried tofu, water spinach, squid and prawns. Cook for 1 to 2 minutes, then divide the mixture into the bowls. Add the broth and season with yen ta fo sauce. The soup should be sweet, salty and sour at the same time. Adjust the seasoning to taste.

Serve with a little of the garlic oil and fried garlic.

Note
The oil and garlic will keep for several months in the refrigerator. The oil can be used to fry vegetables or rice. The garlic can be used to flavour other noodle recipes. If you don't like the taste of fermented red tofu, you can replace it with more ketchup.

| Serves 4 | Preparation 35 minutes | Soaking 45 minutes | Cooking 1½ hours |

Guay Jab

Pork, tofu, egg & rice noodle soup

Guay jab is a soup of Chinese origin, traditionally made from pork offal cooked in a Chinese spiced broth. Its distinct style lies in the triangular shape of the noodles, which roll up to form small cylinders when cooked.

400 g (14 oz) rice flake noodles
4 spring onion stems
6 sprigs of coriander (cilantro)
Chillies in vinegar (optional)

Broth
4 eggs
6 cubes of fried tofu
600 g (1 lb 5 oz) pork belly with rind (or shoulder)
25 g (1 oz) fresh ginger
6 large garlic cloves
½ onion
3 star anise
1 cinnamon stick
2 tablespoons soy sauce
1 tablespoon dark soy sauce
1 tablespoon fish sauce
25 g (1 oz) raw sugar
1 level teaspoon salt
1.5 litres (6 cups) basic broth (recipe page 118) or water

Soak the rice flake noodles in a large container of water for 45 minutes.

Prepare the broth. Bring a saucepan of water to a boil and cook the eggs for 10 minutes so that they are hard boiled. Cut the tofu cubes in half. Cut the pork belly into two large strips. Cut the ginger into strips. Smash the garlic cloves with the back of a knife to release the flavour and remove the skins.

In a Dutch oven, combine all the broth ingredients, except the eggs and tofu. Bring to a boil, skim, lower the heat and allow to simmer for 45 minutes. Add the peeled hard-boiled eggs and continue cooking for 20 minutes. Add the tofu and cook for 5 minutes until heated through. Taste the broth and adjust the seasoning if necessary.

Remove the meat and eggs. Cut the meat into 5 mm (¼ inch) slices and the eggs in half. Chop the spring onion stems and coriander.

Bring a large saucepan of water to a boil and tip in the rice flake noodles. They will roll up. As soon as they start to rise to the surface, taste to check the cooking: the noodles should be slightly al dente. Drain and divide into four bowls.

Add the topping (pork, egg, tofu). Pour hot broth over the top. Serve with the spring onion, coriander and chillies in vinegar (if using).

Chillies in vinegar
Slice small Thai chillies and cover them with white vinegar. Marinate for at least 1 hour in a jar before use. Store them in the tightly sealed jar at room temperature.

| Serves 4 | Preparation 20 minutes | Cooking 2¼ hours |

Bami Phet

Duck with wheat noodles

8 Batavia or butter lettuce leaves
600 g (1 lb 5 oz) fresh wheat noodles
80 g (2¾ oz) bean sprouts
3 spring onion stems
3 chillies in vinegar (recipe page 130)

Broth
1 cinnamon stick
2 star anise
1 tablespoon coriander seeds
1 onion
3 garlic cloves
50 g (1¾ oz) fresh galangal
1.5 litres (6 cups) basic broth (recipe
    page 118) or water
4 duck legs
40 g (1½ oz) palm sugar
2 tablespoons soy sauce
2 tablespoons oyster sauce
10 coriander (cilantro) stems
    (without leaves)
Pepper

Fried garlic
6 large garlic cloves
80 ml (⅓ cup) vegetable oil

Toast the cinnamon, star anise and coriander seeds in a dry frying pan for about 5 minutes.

Cut the onion in half. Smash the 3 garlic cloves with the back of a knife to release the flavour and remove the skins. Cut the galangal into strips.

Prepare the fried garlic. Finely chop the 6 garlic cloves. Heat the oil in a small saucepan over a medium heat and fry the garlic, stirring regularly. As soon as it begins to colour, turn off the heat. The garlic will continue to cook in the hot oil. Strain. Store the oil and fried garlic in separate containers.

Pour the broth into a Dutch oven, add the toasted spices, duck legs, onion, garlic cloves, galangal, sugar, sauces and coriander stems. Season with pepper. Bring to a boil, skim if necessary, and simmer over a low heat for 2 hours. Add a little water halfway through cooking if necessary. The duck legs must remain fully covered by the broth. At the end of cooking, the flesh should separate with a fork. Degrease the broth by removing the fat from the surface using a ladle.

Divide the lettuce leaves (shredded or whole) into four bowls.

Bring a saucepan of water to a boil and cook the noodles until al dente, following the pack instructions or to your liking. Ten seconds before the end of cooking, add the bean sprouts to blanch them. Drain everything and divide into the bowls. Add a duck leg. Pour over the hot broth through a sieve.

Chop the spring onion and add into the bowls. Sprinkle with fried garlic, and add 1 teaspoon of chopped chillies in vinegar.

Tip
The soup can be prepared in advance. Keep the broth and duck legs in the refrigerator. To serve, just heat them through and cook the noodles.

| Serves 6 | Preparation 15 minutes | Cooking 30 minutes |

Mee Kati

Pork & coconut
noodle soup

Traditionally, this soup contains tender pork rind cut into pieces. This is a version made from pork mince that contains less protein. At the end of cooking, we add beaten eggs that are drizzled on top of the boiling soup.

900 g (2 lb) fresh rice noodles,
    5 mm (¼ inch) thick
½ bunch of spring onions
250 g (9 oz) bean sprouts
½ bunch of mint

Soup
5 lemongrass stalks
4 red Asian shallots
6 tablespoons vegetable oil
50–100 g (1¾–3½ oz) red curry paste
    (recipe page 86 or store-bought)
500 g (1 lb 2 oz) pork mince
    (belly, shoulder)
3 tablespoons fermented salted
    soy beans (optional)
500 ml (2 cups) water
100 g (3½ oz) raw sugar
½ teaspoon salt
2 tablespoons fish sauce
800 ml (3¼ cups) coconut milk

Prepare the soup. Cut the lemongrass stalks into three sections and bruise them with a rolling pin to release the flavour. Slice the shallots. In a Dutch oven, heat the oil over a medium heat and fry the shallots, then add the curry paste and cook for 2 minutes, stirring. Add the meat, fermented salted soy beans and lemongrass. Stir vigorously. Add the water, sugar, salt and fish sauce. Bring to a simmer and cook for 10 minutes.

Pour in the coconut milk and simmer for 15 minutes. Taste and adjust the seasoning if necessary. The soup should be nice and spicy.

Bring a saucepan of water to a boil and cook the noodles in several batches for about 1 minute each batch. Remove the noodles using a skimmer and divide them into six bowls. Immediately pour over the hot soup to prevent the noodles from sticking together. Slice the spring onion and sprinkle over, along with the bean sprouts and mint leaves.

Choosing a cut of meat
Pork belly has more fat than shoulder but is juicier when cooked, whereas pork shoulder is leaner but drier when cooked.

Variation
Replace the fresh rice noodles with dried rice noodles. To use dried noodles, soak them beforehand for 40 minutes in a large bowl of cold water.

| Serves 6 | Preparation 40 minutes | Cooking 35 minutes |

Khanom Jeen Nam Ya

Fish & coconut noodle soup

This dish dates back to the era of the kingdom of Ayutthaya (between the fourteenth and eighteenth centuries). Khanom jeen means 'Chinese noodles' (rice noodles is assumed) and nam ya is the fish curry. Khanom jeen nam ya is a very popular dish, especially in the southern regions of the country. It is often served at family meals, religious ceremonies and traditional festivals.

3 carrots
1 small Batavia or butter lettuce
½ bunch of mint
½ bunch of coriander (cilantro)
200 g (7 oz) bean sprouts
400 g (14 oz) rice vermicelli
   (e.g. Wai Wai brand)
2–3 limes

Soup

1 kg (2 lb 4 oz) mackerel
600 ml (2⅓ cups) water
50 g (1¾ oz) fresh galangal
50 g (1¾ oz) fingerroot (krachai)
4 lemongrass stalks
4 tablespoons coconut or vegetable oil
40–80 g (1½–2¾ oz) red curry paste
   (recipe page 86 or store-bought)
10 lime leaves
30 g (1 oz) anchovies in oil
15 g (½ oz) raw sugar
1 teaspoon salt
1 tablespoon fish sauce
600 ml (2⅓ cups) coconut milk

Prepare the soup. Place the mackerel in a saucepan with 500 ml (2 cups) cold water, bring to a low simmer and cook for 10 minutes. Remove the mackerel with a skimmer and keep the broth. Allow the fish to cool, then remove the flesh without the skin.

Cut the galangal into strips. Slice the fingerroot and process well with 100 ml (scant ½ cup) water. Cut the lemongrass stalks into three sections and bruise them with a rolling pin to release the flavour.

In a large Dutch oven, heat the oil over a medium heat and fry the curry paste for 5 minutes. Add the blended fingerroot, lemongrass, galangal, lime leaves, drained anchovies, sugar, salt, fish sauce, mackerel broth and flesh. Simmer for 10 minutes. Pour in the coconut milk and cook for a further 10 minutes. Taste and adjust the seasoning if necessary.

Grate the carrots and shred the lettuce. Pick the leaves from the mint and coriander and add to a platter with the bean sprouts.

Cook the rice vermicelli according to the pack instructions. Drain and rinse well under cold water. Drain again. Take a small amount of vermicelli, roll into a nest and squeeze between your hands to remove the water. Place in a colander or sieve.

To serve, each guest takes a bowl and their choice of vermicelli and crudités. Then drizzle the hot soup over the top. Sprinkle with herbs and add a drizzle of lime juice.

| Serves 6 | Preparation 1 hour | Cooking 1¼ hours |

Khao Soi

Chicken curry noodle soup

Khao soi is an iconic dish from Chiang Mai. You can recognise it by the fried noodles on top of the soup. It is believed that the dish was created through the influence of the Chin Haw community from Yunnan, as well as Burmese traders who travelled along the Silk Road.

500 ml (2 cups) oil for frying
660 g (1 lb 7 oz) fresh wheat noodles
6 spring onion stems
2 red Asian shallots (optional)
200 g (7 oz) pickled mustard greens
(optional)
Lime juice (to taste)

Soup

3 lemongrass stalks
70 g (2½ oz) fresh galangal
3 chicken Marylands (thigh and
drumstick)
2 onions
4 garlic cloves
1 teaspoon coriander seeds
3 cardamom pods
6 tablespoons coconut oil or vegetable oil
25–50 g (1–1¾ oz) red curry paste (recipe
page 86 or store-bought)
1 level tablespoon Madras curry powder
1 level teaspoon ground turmeric
2 bay leaves
1 litre (4 cups) water
25 g (1 oz) palm sugar
3 tablespoons fish sauce
1 level teaspoon salt
600 ml (2⅓ cups) coconut milk

Cut the lemongrass stalks into three sections and bruise them with a rolling pin to release the flavour. Cut the galangal into strips. Cut the chicken thighs at the joint to make six pieces. Peel and slice the onions and garlic.

Toast the coriander seeds in a dry frying pan for a few seconds over a medium heat. Grind the coriander seeds and cardamom pods with a pestle.

In a Dutch oven, heat half the oil over a low heat. Sauté the onions and garlic for about 20 minutes, until they are soft and caramelised. Process everything together until a smooth paste forms. Set aside (not in the Dutch oven).

In the same Dutch oven, heat the remaining oil over a medium heat. Fry the red curry paste and ground spices for 3 minutes. Add the onion and garlic paste, lemongrass, galangal, bay leaves and chicken pieces. Add the water to cover. Add the sugar, fish sauce and salt. Bring to a boil, lower the heat and allow to simmer for 35 minutes. Add a little more water if necessary. Pour in the coconut milk and cook for a further 10 to 15 minutes. Taste and adjust the seasoning if necessary.

In a frying pan, heat the oil for frying. Shake 60 g (2¼ oz) of the wheat noodles in a colander to remove excess flour. Gently place small piles of noodles into the hot oil. Be careful of spills and splattering. Fry for just 1 minute: the noodles should be golden brown. Remove and drain on paper towel.

Bring a large saucepan of water to a boil and cook the remaining wheat noodles according to the pack instructions, so that they are slightly al dente. Cook them in several batches, if needed. Drain and divide into six bowls. Add one piece of chicken per person. Pour hot soup over the top. Slice the spring onion and sprinkle over, along with the shallot and mustard greens (if using). Top with a handful of fried noodles. Each guest adds a dash of lime juice before eating.

Soups — 139

| Serves 8 | Preparation 40 minutes | Cooking 10 minutes |

Sukiyaki

Japanese fondue

Japanese-style sukiyaki started to appear in Thailand in the 1980s, when tourism between the two countries began to develop. The Thai version has adapted to local tastes and ingredients, but what really sets it apart is its sweet-and-sour sauce, made from fermented red soy paste, sugar, fish sauce and rice vinegar. At home we make a tamarind-based version, which is more acidic, lighter and easier to make. The list of ingredients is just a suggestion. You can choose what you like – there are no hard and fast rules.

200 g (7 oz) bean thread vermicelli
400 g (14 oz) chicken breast
400 g (14 oz) sukiyaki beef (top sirloin, rump, tenderloin)
400 g (14 oz) fish fillet of your choice (mulloway, cod, ling, salmon etc.)
300 g (10½ oz) chrysanthemum leaves, watercress or water spinach
1 small Chinese cabbage
250 g (9 oz) firm tofu
24 raw prawns
400 g (14 oz) spinach leaves
300 g (10½ oz) mushrooms of your choice (button, fresh shiitake, shimeji, oyster mushrooms)
2.5 litres (10 cups) basic broth (recipe page 118)

Tamarind sauce
500 ml (2 cups) boiling water
120 g (4¼ oz) tamarind paste without seeds
70 g (2½ oz) tomato paste (concentrated purée)
130 g (4½ oz) white (granulated) sugar
2 level teaspoons salt
4 tablespoons fish sauce
6 garlic cloves
Toasted sesame seeds
½ bunch of coriander (cilantro)
Fresh chillies (to taste)

Prepare the tamarind sauce. In a bowl, pour the boiling water over the tamarind paste, allow to stand for 10 minutes, then use your hands to mix the paste into the water until dissolved. Strain over a saucepan by pressing the paste down with the back of a spoon to extract a thick juice. Add the tomato paste, sugar and salt. Bring to a boil, remove from the heat and add the fish sauce. Allow to cool before serving in individual bowls. Guests can add crushed garlic, toasted sesame seeds, chopped coriander and chopped chilli, to taste.

Rehydrate the vermicelli for 15 minutes in cold water. Finely slice the chicken and beef. Cut the fish into cubes. Cut the chrysanthemum leaves, watercress or water spinach into three sections. Cut the Chinese cabbage and tofu into even-sized pieces. You can choose to peel the prawns or not (unpeeled, they will add more flavour to the broth; peeled, they will be easier to eat). Arrange all these ingredients as well as the spinach leaves and mushrooms in dishes.

Heat the broth in a Chinese hot pot or a fondue set.

Each guest fills their hot pot strainer scoop and dips it into the boiling broth, then into their bowl of sauce. Add broth or water as you go to ensure there is enough liquid.

The broth will be enriched with all the flavours of the ingredients over the course of the meal. It is customary to drink the remaining broth at the end.

Sukiyaki (recipe page 140)

Stir-fries

| Serves 3 to 4 | Preparation 30 minutes | Soaking 1½ hours | Cooking 15–20 minutes | Step-by-step |

Pad Thai

Pad thai is the Thai national dish. During the economic recession that hit Thailand after the Second World War, Prime Minister Plaek Phibunsongkhram decided to export more rice to reduce the economic deficit. He then began to promote a rice noodle dish that required less precious raw materials to make. This is how pad thai was born.

146 — Stir-fries

300 g (10½ oz) dried rice noodles
 (5 mm/¼ inch wide)
8 raw king prawns or 16 raw large
 peeled prawns
150 g (5½ oz) pork or chicken mince
1 tablespoon soy sauce
1 tablespoon fish sauce
40 g (1½ oz) preserved radish (in a sachet)
25 g (1 oz) dried shrimp
2 red Asian shallots
6 garlic scapes or spring onion stems
6 tablespoons vegetable oil
4 eggs
200 g (7 oz) bean sprouts
4 tablespoons chopped roasted peanuts
1 lime
Chilli powder (optional)
Salt

Sauce

70 g (2½ oz) palm sugar
100 g (3½ oz) tamarind concentrate
 (recipe page 255 or store bought)
3 tablespoons fish sauce
1 tablespoon dark soy sauce
50 ml (scant ¼ cup) cold water

Soak the rice noodles for 1½ hours in cold water. Peel the king prawns (or prawns), leaving the head and tail. Season with salt and set aside in the refrigerator. Mix the mince with the soy sauce and fish sauce.

Prepare the sauce. Chop the palm sugar, then combine it with the other sauce ingredients.

Chop the preserved radish. Coarsely chop the dried shrimp. Slice the shallots. Cut the garlic scapes or spring onion stems into three or four sections (**1**).

Heat 1 tablespoon oil in a wok over a medium heat and sear the king prawns for 1 minute on each side. Set aside. If using large prawns, fry for about 2 to 3 minutes.

Heat the remaining oil over a medium heat and fry the shallots with the radish and dried shrimp for 3 to 4 minutes. Add the mince and stir well. When the pork is cooked, after about 5 minutes, increase the heat and add the drained rice noodles. Pour in the sauce (**2**) and mix. When the noodles have absorbed the sauce, taste. If they still need more cooking, add a little water.

Push the noodles to one side of the wok and break the eggs into the wok. Let the whites set slightly and then lightly scramble. Cover them with the noodles. Add the prawns and mix. Remove from the heat. Add the garlic scapes or spring onion stems and bean sprouts. Mix.

Serve with chopped peanuts, a lime wedge and chilli powder (if you like it hot).

Note

If you do not have a large wok, divide the sauce and filling in half and mix it with the noodles in two batches.

Stir-fries

| Serves 2 to 3 | Preparation 30 minutes | Cooking 15 minutes |

Pad See Ew

Stir-fried rice noodles with beef & Chinese broccoli

150 g (5½ oz) tender beef (sirloin, rump)
1 tablespoon soy sauce
350 g (12 oz) Chinese broccoli (gai-lan) or broccoli
4 garlic cloves
400 g (14 oz) fresh rice noodles
4 tablespoons oil
3 eggs
Chillies in vinegar (recipe page 130) (optional)
Pepper

Sauce

1 level tablespoon raw sugar
2 tablespoons oyster sauce
2 tablespoons soy sauce
1 tablespoon fish sauce
1 tablespoon dark soy sauce

Finely slice the beef and season with soy sauce and pepper. Cut the broccoli stalks into slices, and the leaves in half or thirds. Chop the garlic cloves. Separate the noodles.

Prepare the sauce by combining all the sauce ingredients in a bowl.

Heat 1 tablespoon oil in a wok over a high heat and sear the meat for 1 minute, stirring vigorously. Set aside.

Heat the remaining oil over a medium heat and fry the garlic and broccoli for 2 minutes. Push the vegetables to the side and break the eggs in the centre of the wok. Allow them to set before lightly scrambling. Increase the heat to high, add the noodles and pour in the sauce. Stir vigorously to coat the noodles with sauce, then allow to caramelise for a few moments without stirring. Serve immediately with a few chopped chillies in vinegar.

Tip

The secret to all stir-fried noodle dishes is to add small portions at a time. This allows more even temperature and cooking on the wok's surface. It also makes it easier to mix in circular movements.

Variation

You can replace 400 g (14 oz) fresh noodles with 250 g (9 oz) dried noodles. Soak them for 45 minutes in cold water, then blanch for 30 seconds in boiling water. Rinse with cold water and drain before adding to the wok.

| Serves 4 | Preparation 35 minutes | Soaking 45 minutes | Cooking 15 minutes |

Pad Kee Mao

Stir-fried rice noodles with prawns, chilli & Thai basil

Pad kee mao is also known as drunken noodles based on the legend that these spicy Thai noodles should be eaten with an ice-cold beer (or several due to the spiciness of the dish!). To avoid hiding under the table with your tongue on fire, use mild Caribbean chillies (aji dulce) for this recipe as they are very fragrant without the heat. They can be found in the chilled section of Asian supermarkets or in Caribbean grocery stores.

300 g (10½ oz) dried rice noodles, 1 cm (½ inch) wide
300 g (10½ oz) frozen peeled prawns with tails, thawed
1 heaped teaspoon raw sugar
1 tablespoon fish sauce
5 garlic cloves
1 bunch of Thai basil
5 mild chillies (aji dulce) or 2 Thai red chillies
6 tablespoons vegetable oil
Salt and pepper

Sauce
4 tablespoons oyster sauce
3 tablespoons soy sauce
1 tablespoon dark soy sauce
1 tablespoon fish sauce

Soak the rice noodles in a large container of water for 45 minutes.

Split the back of the prawn tails with a knife and remove the vein. Put them in a bowl. Season with salt and pepper, add the sugar and fish sauce. Set aside at room temperature.

Roughly chop the garlic. Pick the leaves from the Thai basil. Slice the chillies.

Prepare the sauce by combining all the sauce ingredients in a bowl.

Heat 2 tablespoons oil in a wok or large frying pan over a medium heat. Fry the garlic. When it starts to brown, add the prawns and chillies. Cook for 1 minute over a high heat, stirring (the prawns will finish cooking with the noodles). Set aside.

Bring a saucepan of water to a boil, blanch the noodles for 30 seconds, drain. Rinse thoroughly with cold water, drain again. Divide all the ingredients in half to fry the noodles in two batches.

Heat 2 tablespoons oil in a wok over a very high heat. Add half the noodles and half the sauce. Mix together. Allow the noodles to absorb the sauce for 2 to 3 minutes. Add half the prawns and continue cooking until no liquid remains in the pan.

Off the heat, add the Thai basil. Set aside in a container. Repeat with the remaining noodles, sauce and prawns. Mix everything together before serving.

Serves	Preparation	Cooking
2 to 3	40 minutes	20 minutes

Raad Na

Rice noodles in sauce

Raad na is a dish of Chinese origin, and the name is short for kway tiaow raad na, meaning 'coated noodles'. Homesick emigrants once cooked it on burners for a meal on the go. Gradually, they began to sell it to the workers and that's how raad na became a very popular street food dish.

400 g (14 oz) fresh rice noodles
250–300 g (9–10½ oz) bok choy
100 g (3½ oz) fresh shiitake or button mushrooms
4 large garlic cloves
4 tablespoons vegetable oil
1 tablespoon dark soy sauce
1 tablespoon soy sauce
3 eggs
1 heaped tablespoon tapioca starch or cornflour
350 ml (scant 1½ cups) water
2 tablespoons oyster sauce
1 heaped teaspoon raw sugar
1 tablespoon fish sauce
Chillies in vinegar (recipe page 130)
Pepper

Marinated meat
150 g (5½ oz) pork tenderloin (or chicken breast or peeled prawns)
1 level tablespoon raw sugar
½ teaspoon salt
1 tablespoon fish sauce
1 level tablespoon tapioca starch or cornflour

Prepare the marinated meat. Slice the pork tenderloin. Put the slices in a bowl with all the seasonings. Set aside at room temperature while preparing the rest.

Separate the rice noodles. Cut the bok choy into even-sized pieces. Slice the mushrooms. Chop the garlic.

Heat the oil in a wok over a medium heat. Fry the garlic. As soon as it is nicely golden, remove it from the oil with a skimmer, leaving the oil in the wok. Set aside in a bowl. Add the noodles to the garlic oil, as well as the soy sauces. Mix well and cook for 2 to 3 minutes over a high heat. Push the noodles to the side and break the eggs in the centre of the wok. Allow the eggs to set before scrambling, then mix together with the noodles. Set aside in a dish and keep warm.

Mix the tapioca starch with a little cold water until combined. Pour the 350 ml (scant 1½ cups) water into the wok. Add the bok choy and mushrooms. Bring to a boil. Add the fried garlic and cook for 3 to 4 minutes. Add the pork, oyster sauce, sugar and fish sauce. Season with pepper. Cook for 2 to 3 minutes. Pour the tapioca starch and water mixture into the wok and stir until the sauce thickens.

Divide the noodles onto plates and top with sauce. Serve with chopped chillies in vinegar.

Variation
You can replace 400 g (14 oz) fresh noodles with 250 g (9 oz) dried rice noodles that are 1 cm (½ inch) wide. Soak them for 45 minutes in cold water, then blanch them for 30 seconds in boiling water. Rinse with cold water and drain before adding to the wok.

| Serves 2 to 4 | Preparation 15 minutes | Soaking 30 minutes | Cooking 15 minutes |

Pad Woon Sen Kai

Stir-fried bean thread noodles with egg

150 g (5½ oz) bean thread vermicelli
3 garlic cloves
1 onion
3 spring onion stems
5 tablespoons vegetable oil
5 eggs
50 ml (scant ¼ cup) water
120 g (4¼ oz) bean sprouts

Sauce
2 tablespoons soy sauce
1 level teaspoon raw sugar
1 heaped tablespoon oyster sauce
Pepper

Soak the vermicelli in cold water for around 30 minutes.

Chop the garlic. Slice the onion and spring onion.

Prepare the sauce by combining the sauce ingredients in a bowl. Season generously with pepper.

Drain the vermicelli and cut in half or thirds.

Heat the oil in a wok or large frying pan over a medium heat. Fry the onion and garlic. When the garlic begins to brown, push everything to one side and break the eggs in the centre of the wok. Allow them to set before scrambling. Increase the heat, add the vermicelli, sauce and water. Continue cooking until the vermicelli have absorbed all the sauce. Taste to check the cooking and seasoning.

Remove from the heat, add the bean sprouts and spring onion. Mix.

This dish is traditionally served with rice.

Serves	Preparation	Cooking
3 to 4	20 minutes	12 minutes

Pad Prik King

Stir-fried green beans with pork & red curry paste

- 300 g (10½ oz) pork tenderloin (or chicken breast or peeled prawns)
- 3 tablespoons vegetable oil
- 3 tablespoons fish sauce
- 500 g (1 lb 2 oz) green beans, tailed
- 20 lime leaves
- 20 g (¾ oz) palm sugar
- 1 level tablespoon red curry paste (recipe page 86 or store-bought)

Cut the tenderloin into 3 mm (⅛ inch) slices. Place in a bowl with 1 tablespoon oil and 1 tablespoon fish sauce. Mix together and set aside at room temperature.

Cut the green beans in half or thirds depending on their length. Remove the central rib from the lime leaves, roll the leaves together, then slice them as thinly as possible. Chop the palm sugar.

Bring a saucepan of water to a boil and immerse the beans in the boiling water for 3 minutes. Reserve 100 ml (scant ½ cup) cooking water, then drain.

Heat 1 tablespoon oil in a wok or large frying pan over a high heat. Sear the meat without stirring it too much for just 1 minute. Remove and set aside. Lower the heat a little, add 1 tablespoon oil and fry the curry paste with the palm sugar for 2 minutes. Add the beans, 2 tablespoons fish sauce and lime leaves. Stir and add a little cooking water reserved from the beans. Cook for 2 to 3 minutes, then add the meat. Pour in a little water if necessary and continue cooking for 2 to 3 minutes. The beans should still be slightly crunchy. Taste to check the seasoning and cooking.

Serve with white rice.

| Serves 4 | Preparation 15 minutes | Cooking 8 minutes |

Pad Horapa Moo

Stir-fried pork mince with Thai basil

The authentic recipe uses holy basil (*Ocimum tenuiflorum*), called krapao in Thai, which is a little hard to find. It has a slightly lemony taste and goes perfectly with the meat. But the recipe made here with Thai basil is just as delicious.

1 large bunch of Thai basil
4 garlic cloves
1 onion
1 long chilli or 2 Thai red chillies
3 tablespoons vegetable oil
500 g (1 lb 2 oz) pork mince (belly, shoulder)
4 fried eggs (optional)

Sauce
2 tablespoons fish sauce
1 heaped teaspoon raw sugar
1 tablespoon soy sauce
¼ teaspoon salt

Pick the leaves from the Thai basil. Chop the garlic. Slice the onion. Slice the long chilli or split the Thai red chillies in half lengthways and remove the seeds (or not, to taste).

Prepare the sauce by combining the sauce ingredients in a bowl.

Heat the oil in a wok or large frying pan over a very high heat. Fry the onion and garlic. As soon as the garlic begins to brown, add the meat and chilli. Stir and crush the meat to break up the pieces. Pour in the sauce and continue cooking for 3 to 5 minutes, until the meat is cooked. Remove from the heat and add all the Thai basil. Stir, taste and adjust the seasoning by adding fish sauce if necessary.

Serve with rice and 1 fried egg per person.

Variation
Pork can be replaced with beef or chicken mince.

Serves	Preparation	Cooking
3 to 4	20 minutes	20 minutes

Pad Phed

Stir-fried duck with red curry, green peppercorns & Thai basil

1 duck breast
1 onion
3 garlic cloves
6 lime leaves
½ red capsicum (pepper)
1 tablespoon red curry paste (recipe page 86 or store-bought)
4 branches of fresh green peppercorns
150 ml (generous ½ cup) coconut milk
3 tablespoons fish sauce
2 tablespoons tamarind concentrate (recipe page 255 or store-bought)
1 teaspoon raw sugar
1 bunch of Thai basil
Salt

Score the duck breast skin with a sharp knife and salt both sides. Place the breast in a wok or frying pan, skin-side down, and melt the fat for about 10 minutes over a medium heat. Allow to cool, then cut into thin strips. Set aside the fat in a bowl.

Slice the onion and garlic. Remove the central rib from the lime leaves. Form a pile, roll them up and slice as finely as possible. Remove the stalk, white parts and seeds from the capsicum and cut into strips.

In the wok, heat 3 tablespoons of duck fat over a medium heat and fry the curry paste for 2 minutes. Add the garlic, onion, green peppercorns, lime leaves and capsicum. Separate the peppercorns if you like, to distribute them in the wok. Pour in the coconut milk, fish sauce, tamarind and sugar. Cook for 5 minutes, then add the duck slices. Stir and stop cooking as soon as the duck is pink. Taste and adjust the seasoning if necessary. Remove from the heat and add the Thai basil leaves.

Serve with white rice.

| Serves 4 | Preparation 20 minutes | Cooking 10 minutes |

Gai Pad King

Stir-fried chicken with ginger & black mushrooms

10 g (¼ oz) dried black mushrooms
400 g (14 oz) chicken breast (or boneless chicken thighs)
1 onion
4 garlic cloves
4 spring onion stems
40 g (1½ oz) fresh ginger
3 tablespoons vegetable oil

Marinade
1 tablespoon oyster sauce
2 tablespoons soy sauce
1 tablespoon dark soy sauce
3 tablespoons water
1 teaspoon raw sugar
Pepper

Rehydrate the mushrooms for 1 hour in cold water.

Cut the chicken into even-sized pieces. Place the chicken in a large bowl with the marinade ingredients. Season generously with pepper. Set aside at room temperature while preparing the rest.

Slice the onion. Chop the garlic. Cut the spring onion stems into three or four sections and the ginger into matchsticks. Drain the black mushrooms, remove the hard parts of the bases if necessary, and chop coarsely.

Heat the oil in a wok or large frying pan over a medium heat. Fry the onion, garlic and ginger for 2 to 3 minutes. Increase the heat, add the black mushrooms, chicken and all the marinade. Cook for 5 minutes, stirring regularly (a little longer for boneless chicken thighs). Add the spring onion and mix. Taste and adjust the seasoning if necessary.

Serve with white rice.

Serves 4 | **Preparation** 20 minutes | **Cooking** 10 minutes

Gai Pad Med Mamuang

Stir-fried chicken with cashews

400 g (14 oz) boneless chicken thighs
   (2 large thighs)
2 tablespoons soy sauce
4 garlic cloves
1 onion
½ red capsicum (pepper)
½ green capsicum (pepper)
3 tablespoons vegetable oil
1 tablespoon cornflour
6 dried red chillies (optional)
125 g (4½ oz) roasted cashews

Sauce
1 tablespoon oyster sauce
1 tablespoon fish sauce
1 tablespoon chilli paste
   (nam prik pao)
1 level tablespoon raw sugar

Cut the chicken into even-sized pieces. Place in a large bowl with the soy sauce and set aside at room temperature.

Chop the garlic. Slice the onion. Remove the stalk, white parts and seeds from the capsicums and cut into cubes.

Prepare the sauce by combining the sauce ingredients in a bowl.

Heat the oil in a wok or large frying pan over a medium heat. Coat the chicken with the cornflour, fry in hot oil for 3 to 4 minutes, then remove. In the same oil, fry the onion, garlic and dried chillies (if using) for 2 minutes. Return the chicken to the pan, add the capsicum and sauce. Continue cooking for 3 to 4 minutes. Taste and adjust the seasoning and cooking time if necessary. Remove from the heat and add the cashews.

Serve with white rice.

Stir-fries — 165

| Serves 4 | Preparation 20 minutes | Cooking 12 minutes |

Pad Priew Wan

Sweet-and-sour tofu with pineapple

½ cucumber
½ pineapple
125 g (4½ oz) cherry tomatoes
1 onion
3 garlic cloves
300 g (10½ oz) firm tofu
50 g (1¾ oz) cornflour
4 tablespoons vegetable oil
100 g (3½ oz) roasted cashews

Sauce
3 tablespoons oyster sauce
5 tablespoons white vinegar or
   rice vinegar
2 tablespoons soy sauce
2 tablespoons sriracha sauce
45 g (1½ oz) white (granulated) sugar

Prepare the sauce by combining the sauce ingredients in a bowl.

Cut the cucumber into half moons on the diagonal, pineapple into even-sized pieces and cherry tomatoes in half. Slice the onion and chop the garlic.

Pat the tofu with paper towel, cut it into even-sized cubes, then roll in the cornflour.

Heat the oil in a wok over a medium heat. Brown the tofu cubes and remove. In the same oil, fry the onion and garlic. When the garlic begins to brown, increase the heat, add the cherry tomatoes, cucumber and pineapple. Mix, return the tofu to the wok and pour in the sauce. Cook for 3 to 4 minutes, stirring gently, until everything is coated with sauce. Remove from the heat and add the cashews. Taste and adjust the seasoning if necessary.

Serve with white rice.

Variation
You can replace the tofu with prawns, chicken or pork.

| Serves 4 | Preparation 10 minutes | Cooking 12 minutes |

Khao Pad Kai

Egg fried rice

Fried rice was originally a way to ensure leftovers did not go to waste. It was made with whatever was on hand, most often eggs and left-over vegetables.

3–4 pearl (baby) onions
4 garlic cloves
400 g (14 oz) cold cooked Thai rice from the previous day (recipe page 114)
5 eggs
4 tablespoons vegetable oil
Salt and pepper

Sauce
1 level teaspoon raw sugar
2 tablespoons soy sauce
1 tablespoon oyster sauce

Slice the white and green parts of the onions, reserving the green part. Chop the garlic.

Prepare the sauce by combining the sauce ingredients in a bowl. Pour the sauce over the cold rice and mix well, separating the grains of rice. Season with pepper.

Break the eggs into a bowl, season with salt and pepper and whisk lightly.

Heat the oil in a wok or large frying pan over a medium heat. Fry the white part of the onions and garlic. When the garlic begins to brown, push it and the onion to one side and pour in the eggs. Allow to set before stirring. Add the rice. Mix and cook for 5 to 7 minutes. Taste and if the rice needs more salt, add a little fish sauce. Remove from the heat and add the green part of the onions.

| Serves 4 | Preparation 20 minutes | Cooking 10 minutes |

Khao Pad Gai Tom Yum

Chicken & lemongrass fried rice

250 g (9 oz) chicken breast
15 lime leaves
4 spring onion stems
400 g (14 oz) cold cooked Thai rice from the previous day (recipe page 114)
4 tablespoons vegetable oil
Salt

Garlic–lemongrass paste
1 lemongrass stalk
4 garlic cloves
1 long red chilli, deseeded
25 g (1 oz) fresh galangal

Sauce
2 tablespoons soy sauce
3 tablespoons fish sauce
1 heaped tablespoon chilli paste (nam prik pao)

Topping
4 fried eggs (optional)
1 lime
½ cucumber
Coriander (cilantro) or basil leaves (optional)
Sweet chilli sauce (optional)

Slice the chicken breast, season with salt and set aside at room temperature.

Prepare the garlic–lemongrass paste. Remove the base and hard outer layers of the lemongrass and roughly slice the centre section. Process it with the garlic, chilli and galangal until a paste forms. Set aside.

Remove the central rib from the lime leaves. Form a pile, roll them up and slice as finely as possible. Slice the spring onion stems.

Combine all the sauce ingredients in a bowl to make the sauce. Add the rice and mix evenly.

Heat the oil in a wok or large frying pan over a medium heat. Fry the garlic–lemongrass paste for 2 minutes. Add the chicken and lime leaves and mix. Tip in the rice and fry for 5 to 7 minutes. Taste and adjust the seasoning if necessary. Remove from the heat and add the spring onions.

Serve with a fried egg, if desired, and a drizzle of lime juice. Garnish with cucumber slices and some chopped coriander or basil leaves and sweet chilli sauce, if desired.

| Serves 6 | Preparation 35 minutes | Cooking 15 minutes |

Khao Pad Sapparot

Pineapple, prawn & cashew fried rice

300 g (10½ oz) frozen raw peeled prawns, thawed
6 garlic cloves
50 g (1¾ oz) fresh ginger
1 small onion
4 spring onion stems
700 g (1 lb 9 oz) cold cooked Thai rice from the previous day (recipe page 114)
1 medium pineapple
6 tablespoons peanut oil
4 eggs
100 g (3½ oz) roasted cashews
Salt and pepper

Sauce
3 tablespoons soy sauce
2 tablespoons fish sauce
1 heaped teaspoon raw sugar

Season the prawns with salt and pepper. Set aside in the refrigerator while you prepare the rest.

Chop the garlic and ginger with a knife. Slice the onion and spring onion stems.

Combine all the sauce ingredients in a bowl to make the sauce. Add the rice, season with salt and mix evenly, separating the grains.

Cut the pineapple lengthways. Remove the pineapple flesh by cutting along the skin without piercing it. Then cut the flesh into slices, remove the hard core and cut all the flesh into cubes. Remove the remaining flesh from the skin with a grapefruit knife, spoon or paring knife.

Heat 2 tablespoons oil in a wok or large frying pan over a high heat. Break in the eggs, cook for 1 minute, then scramble and remove. Add 1 tablespoon oil to the wok and fry the prawns for 2 minutes over a high heat. Remove. Pour 3 tablespoons oil into the wok and when hot, fry the garlic, ginger and onion for 2 minutes. Add the rice, mix and cook for 2 to 3 minutes over a high heat. Add the pineapple and continue cooking for 2 minutes. Add the eggs and prawns, then cook for a further 5 minutes. Season with pepper, taste and adjust the seasoning if necessary. Remove from the heat and add the chopped spring onion and cashews. Serve in the hollowed-out pineapple half.

| Serves 2 | Preparation 15 minutes | Cooking 7 minutes |

Pad Pak Boong Fai Daeng

Water spinach, garlic & chilli stir-fry

Pak boong means 'water spinach' and fai daeng means 'red flame'. For a long time I believed that the name came from the amount of red chillies Thais put in this dish! But the red actually comes from the way cooks throw the water spinach into the hot oil of the wok, causing flames to flare up from the burner. This is why it is called 'stir-fried water spinach with red flames' in Thai.

300 g (10½ oz) water spinach (1 large bunch)
4 large garlic cloves
1–2 Thai red chillies (to taste)
4 tablespoons vegetable oil
1 heaped tablespoon oyster sauce
1 tablespoon fish sauce

Cut the water spinach stems into thirds or quarters depending on the length. Keep the leaves intact; they will wilt during cooking. Slice the garlic. Cut the chillies in half lengthways and remove the seeds.

Heat the oil in a wok or large frying pan over a medium heat. When the oil is hot, add the garlic and chilli. As soon as the garlic begins to brown, stir vigorously and add the water spinach. Add the oyster sauce and fish sauce, mix and cook for 3 to 4 minutes, until the water spinach has wilted. Taste and adjust the seasoning if necessary.

Serve with white rice.

Note
The authentic recipe includes 1 tablespoon fermented salted soy beans. If you decide to use it, reduce the amount of oyster sauce by half.

Serves	Preparation	Cooking
2 to 4	10 minutes	7 minutes

Pad Het Prik Thai Sod

Mushroom, green peppercorn & garlic stir-fry

350 g (12 oz) king oyster mushrooms
3 large garlic cloves
1–2 Thai red chillies (optional)
4 tablespoons vegetable oil
4 branches of fresh green peppercorns
1 tablespoon oyster sauce
1 tablespoon fish sauce

Cut the mushroom stems into rounds or half moons depending on their size and the caps in half or quarters. Slice the garlic. Cut the chilli (if using) in half lengthways, remove the seeds, then slice.

Heat the oil in a wok or large frying pan over a medium heat. Fry the garlic and green peppercorns. When the garlic begins to brown, add the mushrooms, chilli, oyster sauce and fish sauce. Separate the peppercorns if you like, to distribute them in the wok. Cook for about 5 minutes. Taste and adjust the seasoning if necessary.

Serve with white rice.

Serves 4 | Preparation 15 minutes | Cooking 10 minutes

Pad Pak Ruam Mit

Vegetable stir-fry

300 g (10½ oz) broccoli
1 large carrot
200 g (7 oz) fresh shiitake or
   button mushrooms
125 g (4½ oz) fresh baby corn
4 large garlic cloves
4 tablespoons vegetable oil
2 tablespoons oyster sauce
2 tablespoons soy sauce
Pepper

Cut the broccoli florets in half or quarters depending on their size. Cut the carrot into rounds on the diagonal. Slice the mushrooms. Cut the baby corn in thirds or quarters. Slice the garlic.

Heat the oil in a wok or large frying pan over a medium heat. Fry the garlic. Add the carrot, broccoli and mushrooms. Add the oyster sauce and soy sauce. Cook for 4 to 5 minutes. Add the baby corn and cook for 2 minutes. Season with pepper, mix, taste and adjust the seasoning if necessary.

Serve with white rice.

Stir-fries — 179

Meat & seafood

| Serves 4 | Preparation 40 minutes | Marinating 1 hour | Cooking 15 minutes |

Aeb Pla

Fish in banana leaf

In Thailand these fish parcels are cooked over low coals.

500 g (1 lb 2 oz) cod or salmon fillet
(with skin or skinless)
1 pack of banana leaves

Marinade
2 long red chillies
2 lemongrass stalks
5 large garlic cloves
2 red Asian shallots
1 tablespoon fish sauce
1 level teaspoon salt
1 teaspoon ground turmeric
Zest of 1 makrut lime or 1 lime
12 lime leaves

Cut the fish into 1 to 1.5 cm (½ to ⅝ inch) thick slices. Put them in a bowl.

Prepare the marinade. Cut the chillies in half lengthways, remove the seeds, then roughly slice. Remove the base and hard outer layers of the lemongrass and cut the centre section into pieces. Roughly chop the garlic and the shallots. Process the chilli, shallots, garlic, lemongrass, fish sauce and salt. Pour over the fish. Add the turmeric and lime zest. Remove the central rib from the lime leaves, make a pile, roll the leaves together, then slice them as thinly as possible. Add to the fish and mix together. Set aside for 1 hour in the refrigerator.

Clean the banana leaves. Dry them and cut 16 rectangles measuring 11 × 22 cm (4¼ × 8½ inches). If the leaves break, put them in the microwave for 20 seconds to soften and make them more pliable.

Preheat the oven to 200°C (400°F).

Layer two banana leaf rectangles, glossy-side down. Place two or three pieces of fish in the middle. Fold the two sides in towards the centre, overlapping them. Close the parcel by folding the top and bottom sides in. Secure with a toothpick. Repeat the process until all the ingredients are used up.

Bake the parcels for 12 to 15 minutes.

Serve with white rice or glutinous rice.

Meat & seafood — 183

| Serves 4 | Preparation 20 minutes | Cooking 10 minutes |

Pla Neung Manao

Steamed fish with lime, garlic & chilli

**This recipe usually contains a phenomenal amount of green chilli.
Using mild aji dulce chillies gives you the taste of chilli without the heat!**

1 lemongrass stalk
1 whole bass or sea bream (650 g/
   1 lb 7 oz)
6 sprigs of coriander (cilantro)

Sauce
6 garlic cloves
8 aji dulce chillies or 4 Thai green chillies
120 ml (½ cup) basic broth (recipe
   page 118) or good-quality
   chicken stock
15 g (½ oz) raw sugar
4 tablespoons fish sauce
Juice of 2 limes

Specific equipment
1 steamer large enough to cook the
   whole fish and 1 pack of banana
   leaves or baking paper
Or 1 large wok or 1 large pot that holds
   a steel grill to place the fish on
Otherwise, replace the whole fish
   with bass fillets

Prepare the sauce. Chop the garlic and aji dulce chillies (or thinly slice the Thai green chillies). Heat the basic broth and sugar in a saucepan over a medium heat and reduce for about 10 minutes, until 80 to 100 ml (⅓ to scant ½ cup) broth remains. Remove from the heat and add the garlic, chilli, fish sauce and juice of 1 lime to start with. Taste. The sauce should be sour, flavourful, garlicky and salty. Adjust by adding more lime juice if necessary.

Cut the lemongrass stalk into four sections and bruise with a rolling pin to release the flavour. Put the lemongrass inside the belly of the fish. Place the fish in a steamer basket lined with a banana leaf or baking paper. Bring water to a boil in the steamer, then insert the basket and cook the whole fish for 7 minutes (4 minutes for fillets).

Chop the coriander. Place the fish gently onto a serving dish and cover with the sauce. Sprinkle with coriander and serve with white rice.

Mok Pla folding

Step-by-step

Using a large bowl as a template, cut out eight circles about 17 cm (6½ inches) in diameter (**1**). Wash, then dry the leaves. Layer two circles, making sure to place one circle with the veins running horizontally on top of another with the veins running vertically. Take the edge of the circle, and form a fold by pinching (**2**).

Use a toothpick to hold the fold (**3**), which should be about 4 cm (1½ inches) (the depth of your basket). Repeat the process on the opposite side (**4**). Repeat the process on the remaining two edges (**5**).

Meat & seafood — 187

Serves 4	Preparation 40 minutes	Marinating 1 hour or overnight	Cooking 15 minutes

Mok Pla

Fish & coconut milk curry

500 g (1 lb 2 oz) cod fillet
1 pack of banana leaves
8 large Chinese cabbage leaves
1 bunch of Thai basil
¼ red capsicum (pepper) (optional)

Marinade
6 lime leaves
40 g (1½ oz) red curry paste (recipe
    page 86 or store-bought)
½ teaspoon salt
1 heaped teaspoon raw sugar
1 tablespoon fish sauce
2 eggs
125 ml (½ cup) coconut milk

Coconut sauce
50 ml (scant ¼ cup) coconut milk
1 teaspoon cornflour

Remove the bones from the fish. Pat the flesh dry, then cut into even-sized pieces.

Prepare the marinade. Remove the central rib from the lime leaves. Form a pile, roll them up and slice as finely as possible. Combine the red curry paste, salt, sugar, fish sauce, eggs and coconut milk in a bowl. Add the lime leaves and stir for about 5 minutes with a wooden spatula, until the mixture becomes creamy and slightly sticky.

Add the fish pieces and mix again with a spatula. Allow to stand for at least 1 hour in the refrigerator, ideally overnight.

Prepare the banana leaf baskets (see page 186). Slice the Chinese cabbage leaves. Bring a saucepan of water to a boil, immerse the cabbage leaves and blanch them for 4 minutes. Squeeze them using your hands to remove all the water.

Prepare the coconut sauce. Heat the coconut milk and cornflour in a saucepan over a low heat, stirring constantly. Stop cooking as soon as the mixture thickens. Set aside.

Fill the bottom of the banana leaf baskets with cabbage and some Thai basil leaves. Then divide the fish into the baskets.

Bring water to a boil in a steamer, then place the trays in the steamer basket and cook for 10 minutes.

Garnish with a little coconut sauce, a few strips of capsicum (if using) and a Thai basil leaf. Serve with white rice.

| Serves 2 | Preparation 20 minutes | Cooking 12 minutes |

Pla Tod Yam Mamuang

Fried sea bream & mango salad

If you can't find a green mango from Southeast Asia, replace it with a green, hard Kent mango (the most common variety) that shows no signs of ripeness. What is important in this recipe is the acidity of the fruit to counterbalance the fat from the frying.

1 whole sea bream (500 g/1 lb 2 oz)
500 ml (2 cups) oil for frying
Salt

Mango salad
1 green mango
1 red Asian shallot
1 red chilli
2 tablespoons raw sugar
3 tablespoons fish sauce
Juice of 1½ limes
2 tablespoons roasted peanuts
A few coriander (cilantro) leaves

Prepare the salad ingredients. Grate the mango with a papaya grater; otherwise, cut into thin strips, then cut the strips into matchsticks. Finely slice the shallot and chilli.

Combine the sugar, fish sauce and lime juice in a bowl.

Wipe the sea bream. Make three cuts on each side. Salt the inside and both sides.

Heat the oil in a large frying pan over a medium heat. When the oil is hot, gently place the fish in the pan and fry for 5 to 6 minutes on each side. Remove and drain on paper towel.

Mix the mango, shallot, chilli, sauce and roasted peanuts.

Serve the sea bream covered with the mango salad, or with the salad on a separate plate. Sprinkle with coriander leaves. Serve with glutinous rice or white rice.

| Serves 2 | Preparation 20 minutes | Cooking 12 minutes |

Pla Sam Rot

Crispy fish with three-flavour sauce

To present the fish in the traditional Thai way, ask the fishmonger for the sea bream carcass. You simply need to fry the carcass for 8 minutes in a large frying pan, then place it under the pieces of fish fillet.

400 g (14 oz) sea bream fillets
50 g (1¾ oz) plain (all-purpose) flour
300 ml (1¼ cups) oil for frying

Three-flavour sauce
1–2 Thai red chillies (to taste)
6 sprigs of coriander (cilantro)
4 garlic cloves
60 g (2¼ oz) palm sugar
2 tablespoons oil
3 tablespoons fish sauce
3 tablespoons tamarind concentrate
   (recipe page 255 or store-bought)
50 ml (scant ¼ cup) water

Prepare the three-flavour sauce. Deseed the chillies, if desired. Pick the leaves from the coriander and set aside, then finely slice the stems. Peel the garlic. Pound the chilli, coriander stems and garlic in a mortar until a paste forms.

Coarsely chop the palm sugar.

Heat the 2 tablespoons oil in a saucepan over a high heat. Fry the chilli paste for 1 to 2 minutes. Add the sugar, fish sauce, tamarind and water. Reduce for 3 to 4 minutes over a medium heat. The sauce should coat the back of a spoon. Taste: the three flavours of this dish are sour from the tamarind, sweet from the palm sugar and salty from the fish sauce. Adjust the seasoning if necessary.

Pat dry the fish fillets. Cut them into even-sized pieces, then roll in the flour.

Heat the frying oil in a saucepan or large frying pan over a high heat. Immerse the pieces of fish in the hot oil for 3 to 4 minutes, until golden brown. Drain on paper towel.

Heat the sauce and pour over the pieces of fish. Sprinkle with coriander leaves. Serve with white rice.

| Serves 4 | Preparation 20 minutes | Soaking 10 minutes | Cooking 8 minutes |

Pla Muk Yad Sai

Stuffed squid

4 cleaned squid with tentacles (about 12 cm/4½ inch tubes)
3 sprigs of mint
2 sprigs of coriander (cilantro)

Filling
20 g (¾ oz) bean thread vermicelli
½ onion
2 garlic cloves
8 sprigs of coriander (cilantro)
300 g (10½ oz) pork mince
1 tablespoon soy sauce
1 teaspoon raw sugar
½ teaspoon salt
Pepper (to taste)

Sauce
1 garlic clove
1–2 Thai red chillies (to taste)
Juice of 1 lime
1 teaspoon salt
1 heaped tablespoon raw sugar
2 tablespoons fish sauce

Soak the vermicelli in a large bowl of cold water for 10 minutes.

Prepare the sauce. Chop the garlic. Slice the chillies. Combine all the ingredients in a bowl.

Prepare the filling. Drain the vermicelli and chop coarsely. Slice the onion. Chop the garlic and coriander. Combine all the ingredients. Gently fill the squid, leaving a 3 cm (1¼ inch) gap at the top. If air bubbles form, prick the tube with a toothpick and expel the air. Insert the tentacles into the tube, then insert a toothpick to hold everything together. Gently make a few incisions on the squid.

Place the squid in a steamer basket lined with a sheet of baking paper. Bring water to a boil in a steamer, then insert the steamer basket and cook for 8 minutes.

Place the squid on a serving dish. Top with the sauce and sprinkle with chopped mint and coriander.

Serve with white rice.

| Serves 6 | Preparation 20 minutes | Soaking 30 minutes | Cooking 12 minutes |

Ob Woon Sen

Prawns with vermicelli

250 g (9 oz) bean thread vermicelli
8 garlic cloves
80 g (2¾ oz) fresh ginger
1 bunch of coriander (cilantro)
1 bunch of spring onions
4 tablespoons oyster sauce
4 tablespoons soy sauce
6 tablespoons peanut oil
200 ml (generous ¾ cup) basic broth
    (recipe page 118) or water
Pepper

Marinated prawns
16 frozen king prawns, thawed
2 tablespoons oyster sauce
2 tablespoons soy sauce
2 tablespoons peanut oil

Soak the vermicelli in a large bowl of cold water for around 30 minutes.

Marinate the prawns. Mix them with oyster sauce, soy sauce and oil, season with pepper and set aside in the refrigerator while preparing the rest.

Peel and smash the garlic cloves with the back of a knife and remove the skin. Peel the ginger and cut into thin slices. Pick the leaves from the coriander. Cut the spring onion into approximately 4 cm (1½ inch) lengths.

Drain the vermicelli, then season with oyster sauce, soy sauce and oil. Season generously with pepper.

Line the bottom of a Dutch oven with spring onion to prevent the vermicelli from sticking to the dish. Add the ginger, coriander, garlic and vermicelli. Pour in the broth. Place the prawns on top with the marinade. Cover and cook for about 10 to 12 minutes over a medium heat. The dish is ready when the prawns are nicely pink and the vermicelli is soft.

Serve with white rice. If you want to serve the dish without rice, remove 1 tablespoon oyster sauce and 1 tablespoon soy sauce when seasoning the vermicelli.

| Serves 6 | Preparation 20 minutes | Cooking 4¼ hours |

Kha Moo Palo

Five-spice pork knuckle

Rice with pork knuckle is a very popular everyday dish in Thailand. It is found everywhere on street market stalls. Thais eat this dish with a sauce made from white vinegar, crushed garlic and sliced chilli.

50 g (1¾ oz) fresh ginger
2 onions
1 head garlic
1 pork knuckle (about 2 kg/4 lb 8 oz)
4 star anise
4 cloves
1 large cinnamon stick
6 bay leaves
1 heaped teaspoon Sichuan pepper
1 level teaspoon whole white peppercorns
2 tablespoons dark soy sauce
6 tablespoons soy sauce
60 g (2¼ oz) palm sugar or raw sugar
30 g (1 oz) salt
330 ml (1⅓ cups) light/blond beer
1 bunch of coriander (cilantro)
6 eggs
250 g (9 oz) fried tofu (optional)

Cut the ginger into strips. Cut the onions in half. Smash the garlic cloves with the back of a knife and remove the skin.

Put the pork knuckle into a large pot, cover with cold water and bring to a boil. Blanch for 8 to 10 minutes, then drain. Clean the pot and put the knuckle back in. Add all the ingredients except the coriander, eggs and tofu. Cover the knuckle completely with water and bring to a boil. Skim, lower the heat and simmer for 4 hours, partially covered. Turn the knuckle occasionally during cooking.

Straight after starting cooking, pick the leaves from the coriander. Add the stems to the pot.

Bring a small saucepan of water to a boil and cook the whole eggs for 8 minutes. Then immerse them in cold water before peeling them gently.

After the knuckle has cooked for 3 hours, add the eggs to the broth. After 3½ hours, add the fried tofu (if using). In total, the knuckle should cook for 4 hours, eggs 1 hour and tofu 30 minutes.

Drain the knuckle and cut into slices with the rind. Cut the eggs and tofu in half, if desired. Serve with white rice, coriander leaves and vinegar sauce, if desired. You can pour the reduced broth on top of the rice.

Vinegar sauce
Mix 2 cloves of crushed garlic with 2 sliced Thai green chillies and a pinch of salt. Cover with white vinegar. Marinate for at least 1 hour in a jar before use. Store them in the tightly sealed jar at room temperature.

| Serves 6 | Preparation 40 minutes | Cooking 1 hour |

Khao Man Gai

Rice flavoured with chicken fat

The Chinese from Hainan Province brought this recipe with them when they immigrated to Southeast Asia in the nineteenth century. This dish, also known as 'Hainanese chicken rice', is part of the culinary heritage of several countries, including Singapore and Malaysia. But it is also found in Indonesia, Vietnam and, of course, Thailand, where it is called khao man gai (khao = rice; man = fat; gai = chicken), in other words 'rice with chicken fat'.

Broth
1 bunch of coriander (cilantro)
1 chicken (1.5 kg/3 lb 5 oz) + 2 thighs
80 g (2¾ oz) fresh ginger
5 garlic cloves
1 onion
1 carrot
1 celery stalk
1 level teaspoon coarse salt
1 level teaspoon sugar

Rice
5 garlic cloves
50 g (1¾ oz) fresh ginger
600 g (1 lb 5 oz) jasmine rice
2 tablespoons vegetable oil
All the fat from the broth
1 level teaspoon salt
½ teaspoon ground turmeric
650 ml (2½ cups) broth

Sauce
100 g (3½ oz) fermented salted soy beans (in a jar)
3 garlic cloves
50 g (1¾ oz) fresh ginger
1–2 chillies (according to taste)
50 g (1¾ oz) raw sugar
Juice of ½ lemon
3 tablespoons soy sauce

Side
1 cucumber

Prepare the broth. Pick the leaves from the coriander and set the leaves and stems aside. Separate the thighs from the whole chicken. Cut the four thighs at the joint.

Peel the 80 g (2¾ oz) ginger and cut it into strips. Peel and smash the 5 garlic cloves. Cut the onion in half, then cut the carrot and celery into sections.

In a large Dutch oven, combine the four chicken thighs, ginger, garlic, onion, carrot and celery. Add the salt, sugar and half the coriander stems. Pour in enough water to cover and bring to a boil. Skim the foam, taking care not to remove the fat. Reduce the heat and cook for 15 minutes. Add the chicken (with the breasts still attached to the carcass). Pour in a little water to immerse the chicken and continue cooking for 20 minutes. Turn off the heat and allow to cool. Collect all the fat on the surface of the broth.

Prepare the rice. Peel and smash the 5 garlic cloves. Peel the 50 g (1¾ oz) ginger and cut it into strips. Rinse and drain the rice. Heat the oil in a large frying pan over a medium heat. Add the garlic and ginger and fry for 2 minutes, then add the drained rice. Cook the rice for 3 to 4 minutes until translucent, then add all the fat from the broth, the salt and turmeric. Mix well. Transfer the rice into the bowl of a rice cooker and add the broth and remaining coriander stems, then start cooking (see page 114).

Prepare the sauce. Process the fermented salted soy beans. Peel and crush the 3 garlic cloves. Grate the 50 g (1¾ oz) ginger. Slice the chillies. Combine all the ingredients.

When you are ready to eat, heat the chicken in the remaining broth, then take the breasts and cut them into pieces. Leave the thighs as they are or remove the flesh. Serve the rice with the chicken, sauce and broth in separate bowls. Sprinkle with coriander leaves. Serve with cucumber cut in half moons.

| Serves 6 | Preparation 30 minutes | Cooking 14 minutes |

Crying tiger

Grilled marinated beef & tamarind sauce

There are several legends associated with the name of this dish. One claims that the piece of meat used is so tender that the tiger cries with pleasure while eating it. A second claims that the sauce is so spicy that the tiger cries with pain while eating it. A third suggests that the recipe uses the most tender pieces of meat and only the offcuts remain, which makes the tiger cry with sadness.

7 tablespoons fish sauce
1 tablespoon soy sauce
2 prime rib steaks (500 g/1 lb 2 oz each)
25 g (1 oz) raw glutinous rice or raw jasmine rice
3 spring onion stems
2 red Asian shallots
6 sprigs of coriander (cilantro)
1 tablespoon vegetable oil
120 g (4¼ oz) tamarind concentrate (recipe page 255 or store bought)
1 teaspoon chilli powder (to taste)
Juice of 1 lime

Palm sugar syrup
100 g (3½ oz) palm sugar
50 ml (scant ¼ cup) water

Prepare the syrup. Coarsely chop the palm sugar. Add the palm sugar and water in a saucepan. Heat for 5 minutes over a medium heat, until a thick syrup forms.

Combine 1 tablespoon palm sugar syrup, 2 tablespoons fish sauce and the soy sauce in a bowl. Pour the mixture over the meat and marinate at room temperature while preparing the rest. Turn the meat from time to time.

Toast the rice in a small dry frying pan over a medium heat. When golden brown, grind it with a pestle or in a coffee grinder. It should still have some texture. Slice the spring onion stems and shallots and pick the leaves from the coriander.

Heat the oil in a large frying pan over a high heat. Grill the steaks for 1 to 2 minutes on each side, for rare cooking. Set aside for 5 minutes on a wire rack.

Combine the tamarind concentrate, 3 tablespoons palm sugar syrup and 5 tablespoons fish sauce in a bowl. Add the chilli powder and half the lime juice. Mix, then taste: the sauce should be tangy and slightly sweet. Adjust the amount of sugar, fish sauce or lime juice if necessary. When ready to serve, add half the spring onion and 2 tablespoons of toasted ground rice.

Cut the meat into slices. Sprinkle with shallot, the remaining spring onion and 1 tablespoon toasted ground rice. Coat the meat with the sauce, or serve it separately. The dish can be served with white rice or glutinous rice.

Tip
If you have left-over palm sugar syrup, store it in a jar in the refrigerator. It can be used like maple syrup.

| Serves 4 | Preparation 20 minutes | Marinating Overnight | Cooking 40 minutes |

Gai Yang

Grilled chicken with lemongrass

4 chicken Marylands (thigh and
   drumstick)
Pepper

Marinade
4 lemongrass stalks
40 g (1½ oz) fresh ginger
5 garlic cloves
4 tablespoons raw sugar
4 tablespoons fish sauce

Prepare the marinade. Remove the base and hard outer layers of the lemongrass and roughly slice the centre section. Peel and coarsely chop the ginger. Process the peeled garlic, ginger, lemongrass, sugar and fish sauce in a food processor.

Cut the chicken thighs at the joint. Put them in a dish and pour over the marinade. Season generously with pepper. Massage the marinade into the chicken. Cover with plastic wrap and marinate overnight in the refrigerator.

Preheat the oven to 200°C (400°F).

Place the chicken on a baking tray, skin-side down, and bake for 40 minutes. Turn the chicken halfway through cooking to allow the skin to brown.

Serve with glutinous rice and papaya salad (recipe page 48).

| Serves 4 | Preparation 20 minutes | Cooking 1½ hours |

Moo Wan

Caramelised pork

800 g (1 lb 12 oz) pork belly with rind
    (or shoulder)
80 g (2¾ oz) fresh ginger
2 red Asian shallots
6 large garlic cloves
½ bunch of coriander (cilantro)
100 g (3½ oz) white (granulated) sugar
100 ml (scant ½ cup) soy sauce
1 teaspoon crushed black pepper

Cut the pork into even-sized pieces. Peel and cut the ginger into thin slices. Thinly slice the shallots. Smash the garlic cloves with the back of a large knife and remove the skin. Chop the coriander.

In a Dutch oven, heat the sugar over a medium heat until a light caramel forms. Deglaze with the soy sauce. Add the pork, garlic, shallot, ginger and pepper. Mix and add water to cover. Cook for 30 minutes over a low heat. Remove the lid and continue cooking for about 1 hour: the sauce should be well reduced and coat the meat.

Remove from the heat and add all the chopped coriander. Mix and serve with white rice.

Serves 6 | Preparation 1 hour | Resting 24 hours | Cooking 20–35 minutes

Sai Oua

Thai sausage

Sausage meat
75 g (2½ oz) lemongrass stalks
100 g (3½ oz) red Asian shallots
15 g (½ oz) lime leaves
40 g (1½ oz) red curry paste (recipe page 86 or store-bought)
1 heaped tablespoon fish sauce
8 g (¼ oz) salt
20 g (¾ oz) sugar
500 g (1 lb 2 oz) pork shoulder or neck
500 g (1 lb 2 oz) fat rindless pork belly

To shape and cook
2 metres (79 inches) pork casing
3 tablespoons oil

Specific equipment
1 sausage funnel

1

2

3

210 — Meat & seafood

Step-by-step

Remove the base and hard outer layers of the lemongrass. Slice the centre of the lemongrass and shallots into even-sized pieces. Remove the central rib from the lime leaves. Form a pile, roll them up and slice as finely as possible. (**1**).

Process the lemongrass until finely chopped. Then add the shallots and process again. Combine the curry paste and fish sauce in a bowl until blended. Add the salt and sugar. If the meat has not been minced by the butcher, cut the meat into pieces and put them through a mincer, alternating lean and fat pieces. Use a wide holeplate to get coarse mince. Mix all the sausage meat ingredients (**2**) by hand for at least 5 minutes to evenly distribute the curry paste and spices. Cover with plastic wrap touching the surface of the meat and set aside in the refrigerator while preparing the casings.

Rinse the casing thoroughly, then run cold water through it to facilitate stuffing and check that the casing is intact. Drain a casing while keeping it moist, then thread it onto the sausage funnel. Allow the casing to protrude by 10 cm (4 inches). Tie a knot.

Fill the funnel with sausage meat and start pushing it into the casing as evenly as possible (**3**). Prick regularly with a toothpick or needle to expel the air (**4**). The casing must not be too tight to prevent it from bursting during filling or cooking. When the sausage is about 15 cm (6 inches) long, smooth it with your hands to see if it is even. Prick the spots where air holes have formed, then close the sausage by tying a knot. Repeat the process until all the ingredients are used up.

Set the sausages aside in the refrigerator for at least 24 hours before cooking or freezing.

if you do not want to bother with the casings, let the sausage meat rest overnight covered with plastic wrap, then shape small oblong koftas in the palm of your hand (**5**).

Pan-fry: heat a drizzle of oil over medium heat and cook the sausages for 20 to 25 minutes, turning them regularly until golden brown.
Oven bake: preheat the oven to 220°C (425°F). Place the sausages on a baking tray or in a dish and bake for 30 to 35 minutes, turning halfway through cooking.

Serve with white rice or glutinous rice.

Meat & seafood — 211

| Serves 4 | Preparation 45 minutes | Soaking 3 hours | Cooking 25 minutes |

Mok Gai

Chicken & dill parcels

Step-by-step

1 tablespoon raw glutinous rice (optional)
500 g (1 lb 2 oz) boneless chicken thighs (about 3 large thighs)
6 spring onion stems
1 bunch of dill
1 pack of banana leaves
8 red chillies (optional)

Marinade
2 lemongrass stalks
1 long chilli
10 g (¼ oz) fresh galangal
4 garlic cloves
2 red Asian shallots
¼ teaspoon salt
2 tablespoons fish sauce
3 tablespoons fermented fish sauce (padaek)

Tip
You can prepare the marinade and soak the rice the day before.

Soak the glutinous rice (if using) in a bowl of cold water for at least 3 hours.

Cut the chicken thighs into even-sized pieces.

Prepare the marinade. Remove the base and hard outer layers of the lemongrass. Cut the long chilli in half lengthways and remove the seeds. Coarsely chop the centre of the lemongrass and long chilli. Process the lemongrass and galangal. Add the garlic, shallots and chilli. Process until a paste forms. Pour over the chicken. Add the salt, fish sauce and fermented fish sauce. Mix together and set aside in the refrigerator.

Cut the spring onion stems into 3 to 4 cm (1¼ to 1½ inch) lengths. Chop the dill. Remove the central rib from the banana leaves. Cut the leaves into eight rectangles measuring approximately 25 × 14 cm (10 × 5½ inches). Keep the offcuts to add a second layer to the parcels. Rinse the cut leaves or soak them in water. Dry them with a clean tea towel. Set aside under the damp tea towel.

Drain the glutinous rice, process it or pound it, then combine it with the chicken, dill and spring onion. Divide the mixture into eight portions.

Add a second layer to a banana leaf rectangle using an offcut. Place three pieces of chicken in the middle and a red chilli (if using). Bring the long edges together in the centre. Fold in the sides, bringing the corners towards the centre (**1–2**). Use a toothpick to secure it all together. Place in a steamer basket. Make the other parcels.

Bring water to a boil in a steamer, then insert the steamer basket and cook for 20 to 25 minutes. Serve with white rice or glutinous rice.

Meat & seafood — 213

Drinks & desserts

Makes around 1.25 litres (5 cups)	Preparation 40 minutes	Soaking Overnight	Cooking 35 minutes

Nam Dao Huu

VEGAN

Homemade soy milk

In Asia, soy milk is often mixed with herbal jelly cubes that can be found in tins at Asian grocery stores ('grass jelly'). The dark-coloured jelly is said to have medicinal properties and its light and refreshing taste is very pleasant during hot weather.

300 g (10½ oz) yellow soy beans
1.5 litres (6 cups) water
25 g (1 oz) raw sugar

Soak the soy beans overnight in cold water.

Use a blender to finely blend the drained beans with the water. Do this in two batches. Pass the mixture through a fine cloth (gauze, cheesecloth, muslin), squeezing well to recover as much concentrated liquid as possible.

Put the sugar and liquid obtained into a saucepan. Cook over a medium heat at a low simmer for 30 to 35 minutes. It is important to properly cook the soy milk because the raw beans are toxic.

Allow to cool completely before drinking. You can further sweeten the milk with maple syrup, coconut or palm sugar or agave syrup.

Serves 2 | Preparation
5 minutes

Gafae Yen

Iced coffee

When I was a child, iced coffee was sold in plastic bags. The seller would slip a straw into the bag so it was poking out of the top and the bag and the straw were held together with an elastic band. You would then hold the bag by the elastic band while sipping the drink. There were also iced coffee delivery drivers, who would hang the bags of iced coffee from the handlebars of their scooters, the bags bouncing back and forth in Bangkok's crazy stop-start traffic.

60 g (2¼ oz) ground coffee
500 ml (2 cups) water
Ice cubes
50 g (1¾ oz) sweetened condensed milk
40 g (1½ oz) unsweetened condensed milk
Sugar (to taste)

Prepare a filter coffee with the indicated amounts of coffee and water. Leave to cool.

Fill two large glasses with ice cubes. Pour in the coffee, then the sweetened condensed milk, which will settle in the bottom of the glass. Then pour in the unsweetened condensed milk.

Stir, taste and add sugar to your liking.

Serves 8 | Preparation 45 minutes | Cooking 10+10 minutes

Step-by-step

Lod Chong Ruam Mit

VEGAN

Three-colour dessert

Lod chong means 'through the hole' – the vermicelli dough goes through the holes of the press – and ruam mit means 'meeting' or 'gathering of friends'. For us, this recipe translates as a combination of our favourite desserts. In Thailand, stands offer a variety of fruits, jellies and seeds that you can choose from. This is a festive dessert that is usually prepared in large quantities for family gatherings.

220 — Drinks & desserts

Iced water
340 g (12 oz) palm seeds (attap) (not to be confused with 'toddy palm's seeds', which are the fruit of another species of palm) (net weight)
230 g (8 oz) jackfruit in syrup (net weight) (optional)
1 litre (4 cups) coconut milk
Ice cubes

<u>Palm sugar syrup</u>
470 g (1 lb 1 oz) palm sugar or raw sugar
200 ml (generous ¾ cup) water

<u>Crunchy rubies (thaptim krob)</u>
340 g (12 oz) tinned water chestnuts (net weight)
Red food colouring (natural if possible)
120 g (4¼ oz) tapioca starch

<u>Pandan vermicelli (lod chong)</u>
150 g (5½ oz) pandan leaves
1 litre (4 cups) water
115 g (4 oz) water chestnut starch
20 g (¾ oz) rice flour
10 g (¼ oz) tapioca starch

<u>Specific equipment</u>
1 potato masher with medium holes

Prepare the palm sugar syrup. Dissolve the palm sugar cakes in the water in a saucepan over a low heat. Set aside.

Prepare the crunchy rubies. Drain and rinse the water chestnuts, then cut them into 6 mm (¼ inch) cubes. In a shallow plate, mix the diced water chestnuts with a little red dye, then roll them in tapioca starch to coat (**1**). Bring a saucepan of water to a boil and sprinkle in the rubies. When they rise to the surface, drain, then set aside in a container with a little palm sugar syrup. Mix to prevent the rubies from sticking together. Add more syrup if necessary.

Make the pandan vermicelli. Wash the pandan leaves, then cut them coarsely. Using a blender, blend the leaves with 1 litre (4 cups) water for a long time to extract all the chlorophyll. Strain the juice obtained through a sieve or gauze. Top up with a little water to obtain 1 litre (4 cups) of juice. Combine the water, chestnut starch, rice flour and tapioca starch in a saucepan. Add the pandan juice and whisk to combine. Prepare a deep pot filled with ice-cold water and the potato masher. Heat the pandan juice mixture over a medium heat, stirring with a spatula. Small lumps will form. Continue cooking and stirring. The mixture will gradually thicken and turn into a slightly sticky batter. When it forms a ball, remove it from the heat. Pour a little batter into the potato masher and press to form vermicelli over the pot of iced water (**2**). Repeat the process until all the batter is used up. Drain the vermicelli.

Rinse and drain the palm seeds. Drain the jackfruit and cut into strips.

In bowls or glasses, arrange the pandan vermicelli, rubies, jackfruit and palm seeds. Add coconut milk and ice cubes, and sweeten to taste by adding the palm sugar syrup.

This dessert is served well chilled. It can also be served as a drink during a meal.

Drinks & desserts

| Serves 4 | Preparation 5 minutes | Cooking 30 minutes |

Kluay Buat Chee

VEGAN

Banana tapioca

This recipe is usually made with a variety of small fragrant bananas that remain firm when cooked (kluay namwah). Sometimes you can find them pre-cooked in the frozen section. Plantain banana is the best alternative because it holds its shape when cooked and is nice and chewy, but it is less fragrant.

70 g (2½ oz) tapioca pearls
1 ripe plantain banana
100 g (3½ oz) palm sugar or raw sugar
250 ml (1 cup) water
400 ml (14 fl oz) tin of coconut milk
1 tablespoon toasted sesame seeds

Bring a saucepan of water to a simmer. Sprinkle in the tapioca pearls and cook for 5 minutes over a low heat, stirring gently. Remove from the heat and allow to cool.

Cut the banana into slices on the diagonal. Coarsely chop the palm sugar.

Add the sugar, water and banana pieces to a saucepan. Cook for 15 minutes over a low heat.

Drain the tapioca pearls. Tip them into the saucepan with the sugar and banana. Pour in the coconut milk and cook for a further 10 minutes. Allow to cool and serve sprinkled with sesame seeds.

Makes	Preparation	Soaking	Cooking
10 crackers	30 minutes	4 hours	4 hours

Khao Taen

VEGAN

Crispy rice crackers with caramel

250 g (9 oz) raw glutinous rice
500 ml (2 cups) oil for frying

Option 1
Light caramel, not very sweet
180 g (6½ oz) palm sugar
50 ml (scant ¼ cup) water

Option 2
Darker caramel
100 g (3½ oz) palm sugar
80 g (2¾ oz) raw sugar
50 ml (scant ¼ cup) water

Soak the glutinous rice in water for 4 hours. Drain and steam for 35 minutes.

On a baking tray lined with baking paper, spread the hot rice out to a 5 mm (¼ inch) thickness and cut out 7 to 7.5 cm (2¾ to 3 inch) discs using a cookie cutter (about 35 g/1¼ oz of rice). Preheat the oven to 80°C (175°F) and bake the rice discs for 3 to 4 hours, turning them occasionally. Once they are completely hard and dry, they can be stored for several weeks in an airtight container at room temperature.

Heat the frying oil to 180°C (355°F) in a saucepan and immerse the rice discs one at a time. They should puff up like rice pops cereal. Flip over to cook the other side. Remove and drain on paper towel.

Make the caramel of your choice: in a saucepan, mix the sugar(s) with the water, heat over a medium heat and cook until the caramel is syrupy, without letting it reduce too much. Spread the crackers with caramel and enjoy.

Drinks & desserts — 225

Serves	Preparation	Resting	Cooking
6 to 8	20 minutes	4 hours or overnight	1¼ hours

Khanom Mo Kaeng

Taro flan

200 g (7 oz) fresh or frozen taro (or cooked chestnuts or red kuri squash)
200 g (7 oz) palm sugar or raw sugar
¼ teaspoon salt
8 eggs
450 ml (1¾ cups) coconut milk
2 pandan leaves or 1 teaspoon vanilla extract or ½ tonka bean, grated (optional)

Cut the taro into even-sized pieces. Steam for 15 minutes to cook.

Coarsely chop the palm sugar. Put it in a bowl with about 3–4 tablespoons of water. Heat for 1 minute in the microwave at 600 W or in a small saucepan. Once the sugar has softened, process it with the cooked taro flesh until you get a smooth purée. Pour into a large metal bowl. Add the salt, eggs, coconut milk and pandan leaves cut into four. Mix gently using your hands, breaking up the eggs, much like kneading a dough. This is the traditional way of mixing this flan without aerating. Once the mixture is nice and smooth, cover with plastic wrap and allow to stand in the refrigerator for at least 4 hours, ideally overnight.

Preheat the oven to 200°C (400°F). Oil a baking dish or cake tin. Strain the mixture through a sieve above the dish. Bake for 20 minutes, then lower the oven temperature to 160°C (315°F) and continue cooking for 30 to 35 minutes.

Allow to cool completely before serving.

| Serves 4 | Preparation 20 minutes | Resting 30 minutes + overnight | Cooking 1 hour |

Sangkaya Fak Thong

Squash flan

- 100 g (3½ oz) palm sugar
- 220 ml (1 scant cup) coconut milk
- 2 pandan leaves or 1 teaspoon vanilla extract (optional)
- 5 eggs
- 1 small kabocha squash or green squash, about the size of a cantaloupe/rockmelon

Coarsely chop the palm sugar. In a saucepan, dissolve the sugar in the coconut milk over a low heat together with the pandan leaves cut into four sections. Allow to cool, then add the eggs and mix. Stand for at least 30 minutes at room temperature.

Open the squash by cutting out a square from the top. Remove the seeds. Strain the coconut-egg mixture, then pour it in to fill the cavity but not quite to the top as the mixture will expand when cooked. Place the squash in a steamer basket with the squash top next to it. Cook for 55 minutes. After 35 minutes, remove the squash top.

Allow to cool completely, then place in the refrigerator for a few hours, ideally overnight. The flan will taste much better the next day. Serve with the squash top in place. Cut the flan into slices and enjoy.

Makes	Preparation	Soaking	Cooking
9 parcels	45 minutes	4 hours	35 minutes

Khao Tom Mut

Sticky rice with banana

Step-by-step

400 g (14 oz) raw glutinous rice
200 ml (generous ¾ cup) coconut milk
150 g (5½ oz) raw sugar
1 pack of banana leaves
4½ bananas

Soak the glutinous rice in a container of cold water for 4 hours. Drain. Line a steamer basket with a cloth or banana leaf scraps, tip in the rice and steam for 20 minutes.

Heat the coconut milk and raw sugar in a saucepan over a low heat. Once the sugar is dissolved, pour over the cooked glutinous rice and mix.

Cut nine rectangles, measuring about 25 × 18 cm (10 × 7 inches), from the banana leaves. Remove the central rib if necessary. Keep the offcuts to add a second layer to the parcels. Wash the leaves, then wipe them dry with a tea towel. Fold the rectangles in half and round off the corners with scissors (**1**).

Cut the bananas in half. Then cut each half banana in half lengthways to facilitate folding.

Take a banana leaf. Add a second layer to the middle section with a banana leaf offcut. Place 1 large tablespoon of glutinous rice in the middle. Add ½ banana (cut in half lengthways). Cover with 1 small tablespoon of rice (**2**). Fold in the long sides, then close the parcel by folding in the other sides (**3**). Place in a steamer basket. Repeat the process with the remaining ingredients.

Bring some water to a boil in a steamer, then insert the steamer basket and cook for 10 minutes. Serve warm.

Drinks & desserts — 231

Serves 4 | Preparation 5 minutes | Resting 2 hours, up to 2 days | Churning 15–30 minutes

Itim Kathi

VEGAN

Coconut ice cream

100 g (3½ oz) palm sugar
600 ml (2⅓ cups) coconut milk
Unsalted roasted peanuts

Specific equipment
Ice cream maker

Coarsely chop the palm sugar. In a saucepan, heat the coconut milk and palm sugar over a low heat until the sugar has dissolved. Remove from the heat and allow to cool completely. Set aside in the refrigerator for a minimum of 2 hours and up to 2 days.

Pour the mixture into an ice-cream maker. Churn until the ice cream has set (allow 15 to 30 minutes, depending on the maker). Enjoy immediately or set aside for 1 hour in the freezer. Serve the ice cream sprinkled with whole peanuts.

This ice cream is delicious served with sticky rice with mango (recipe page 238).

Tip
As this ice cream does not contains stabilisers, it is best to consume it quickly.

| For 1 cake tin (22 cm/8½ inches in diameter × 7 cm/2¾ inches tall) | Preparation 30 minutes | Resting 4½ hours | Cooking 10 minutes |

Woon Phon Lamai

VEGAN

Fruit jelly

Mixed fruit jelly
100 g (3½ oz) tinned lychees with juice (net weight)
125 g (4½ oz) raspberries
125 g (4½ oz) strawberries
480 ml (1¾ cups) liquid (lychee juice + water)
50 g (1¾ oz) white (granulated) sugar
4 g (⅛ oz) agar-agar

Coconut jelly
350 ml (scant 1½ cups) coconut milk
35 g (1¼ oz) white (granulated) sugar
3 g (1/16 oz) agar-agar

Raspberry jelly
250 g (9 oz) raspberry coulis
3 g (1/16 oz) agar-agar

Make the mixed fruit jelly. Cut the lychees into quarters, raspberries in half and strawberries into rounds. Weigh the juice of the lychees and top up with water to obtain 480 ml (1¾ cups) liquid. Pour the liquid into a saucepan, add the sugar and agar-agar, and mix with a whisk. Bring to a boil, lower the heat and cook for 1 to 2 minutes, whisking constantly. Pour a small amount of juice into the cake tin. Allow it to cool slightly before arranging the fruit on top. Pour the remaining juice on top and allow it to set for 15 minutes in the refrigerator.

Prepare the coconut jelly. Mix the coconut milk, sugar and agar-agar in a saucepan with a whisk. Bring to a boil, lower the heat and cook for 1 to 2 minutes, whisking constantly. Allow it to cool slightly before pouring into the tin. Allow to set for 15 minutes in the refrigerator.

Prepare the raspberry jelly. Mix the raspberry coulis and agar-agar in a saucepan with a whisk. Bring to a boil, lower the heat, and cook for 1 to 2 minutes, whisking constantly. Allow it to cool slightly before pouring into the tin. Set aside in the refrigerator for at least 4 hours.

To unmould, run the blade of a knife along the edge. Slide toothpicks between the tin and the jelly and use the knife blade or a spatula to assist. Place a plate on top of the tin and flip over. Wait for the toothpicks to do their work. Be patient, air will get in and allow the jelly to unstick. If you are in a hurry, sit the tin briefly in hot water before turning it over.

You can serve the jelly with coconut ice cream (recipe page 232).

| Serves 8 to 10 | Preparation 40 minutes | Cooking 1 hour (10 × 6 minutes) |

Khanom Chan

Layer cake

Step-by-step

1

2

Khanom chan means 'cake with many layers'. In Thai, there is only one word to designate a layer, floor, level or stratum. My mother translated it as 'layer cake' and the name stuck. This cake must have at least 9 layers. The word 'new' in Thai has the same meaning as 'step', as in 'a step forward'. It is therefore associated with progress and prosperity. This cake is traditionally made for auspicious ceremonies, but these are increasingly rare in Thailand. This means we need to preserve this recipe carefully!

440 g (15½ oz) palm sugar
300 ml (1¼ cups) water
800 ml (3¼ cups) coconut milk
420 g (15 oz) tapioca starch
40 g (1½ oz) rice flour

Pandan extract
120 g (4¼ oz) pandan leaves
150 ml (generous ½ cup) water

Specific equipment
1 cake tin (25 cm/10 inches in diameter × 5 cm/2 inches tall)
1 steamer large enough to hold the tin (if not, divide the quantities by two and use a 20 × 4 cm/8 × 1½ inches cake tin)

Make the pandan extract. Cut the pandan leaves into pieces. Blend them finely in a blender with the water. Pass the mixture through a sieve or gauze over a bowl. Squeeze to recover the concentrated juice. Weigh and add water if necessary, to make up 150 g (5½ oz) pandan extract.

Put the palm sugar and 150 ml (generous ½ cup) of the water in a saucepan. Heat over a low heat. As soon as the sugar has dissolved, remove from the heat and stir in the coconut milk.

Combine the tapioca starch and rice flour in a bowl. Gradually pour the mixture into the coconut milk, stirring with a whisk. Weigh the mixture and divide it into two equal portions in two containers.

In one container, add the 150 g (5½ oz) pandan extract and stir with a whisk. In the other, pour in the remaining 150 ml (generous ½ cup) water and stir with a whisk.

Place the cake tin in the steamer basket. Bring water to a boil, then pour in a layer of the white mixture (**1**). Cover and cook for 6 minutes. Add the same amount of green mixture (**2**). Cover and cook for 6 minutes. Repeat the process, alternating colours to form at least nine layers, finishing with a green layer.

Allow to cool completely before eating. The cake will be better the next day. Cover with plastic wrap on the cake's surface and store at room temperature. If the cake has been stored in the refrigerator, heat it for 20 to 30 seconds in the microwave before serving.

Drinks & desserts

Serves 4 | Preparation 15 minutes | Soaking 4 hours | Cooking 30 minutes

Khao Niao Mamuang

Sticky rice with mango

250 g (9 oz) raw glutinous rice
80 g (2¾ oz) palm sugar
200 ml (generous ¾ cup) coconut milk
1 pinch of salt
2 ripe mangoes

Soak the glutinous rice in a large container of cold water for 4 hours. Drain.

Bring water to a boil in a steamer. Line the basket with a damp tea towel. Add the rice and cook for 15 minutes. Flip the rice over and continue cooking for 10 to 12 minutes (see page 112).

Meanwhile, dissolve the sugar in the coconut milk with the salt in a saucepan over a low heat, without boiling.

When the rice is cooked, transfer it to a container. Allow to cool, then gradually pour in the coconut milk while mixing with a spatula. Stand for 20 minutes at room temperature. The rice should absorb all the liquid.

Cut the mangoes into pieces and serve with the warm rice.

Garnish
You can add a little coconut sauce on top. Dissolve 10 g (¼ oz) palm sugar in 150 ml (generous ½ cup) coconut milk, allow to cool and serve on the sticky rice.

| Serves 8 to 10 | Preparation 20 minutes | Soaking Overnight | Resting Overnight | Cooking 30 minutes |

Khao Niao Dam

VEGAN

Black sticky rice cake

500 g (1 lb 2 oz) raw white glutinous rice
250 g (9 oz) raw black glutinous rice
150 ml (generous ½ cup) water
420 g (15 oz) raw sugar (or 200 g/7 oz
  palm sugar + 220 g/7¾ oz raw sugar)
280 ml (generous 1 cup) coconut cream
50 g (1¾ oz) grated coconut
Toasted sesame seeds

Soak the white glutinous rice and black glutinous rice separately in cold water overnight. The following day, drain the rice (separately).

Add the black rice and the water to a saucepan. Bring to a boil, lower the heat and cook gently, until the rice has absorbed all the water. Taste – the rice should be soft. Extend the cooking if necessary by adding a little water. At the same time, steam the white glutinous rice for 25 to 30 minutes (see page 112). Combine the black rice and white rice in a large container.

Dissolve the sugar in the coconut cream in a saucepan over a low heat. Pour onto the rice. Mix together.

Tip the rice into a large dish. Smooth the top with the back of a spoon. Sprinkle with the grated coconut. The cake should be fully covered to prevent the rice from drying out.

Allow to stand for at least 5 hours at room temperature, ideally overnight. The rice needs to absorb all the liquid and soak up the flavours.

The following day, cut portions and sprinkle with sesame seeds to serve.

Keep the cake refrigerated in an airtight container. Heat for 25 to 30 seconds in the microwave or 5 minutes in a steamer before eating.

| Serves 6 | Preparation 20 minutes | Cooking 1 hour |

Khanom Man Sampalang

VEGAN

Cassava cake

**If you like the chewy texture of Turkish delight, this cake is made for you!
The tapioca starch made from cassava root gives this cake its stretchy texture.
Choose a cassava root that is thin, hard, dry and without stains.**

4 pandan leaves (optional)
200 ml (generous ¾ cup) water (for a texture closer to Turkish delight) or 100 ml (scant ½ cup) water (for a firmer texture)
600 g (1 lb 5 oz) cassava
400 ml (14 fl oz) tin of coconut milk
230 g (8 oz) raw sugar
1 pinch of salt
200 g (7 oz) frozen shredded coconut, thawed, or 80 g (2¾ oz) dry shredded coconut

Specific equipment
1 cake tin (20 cm/8 inches in diameter × 4 cm/1½ inches tall)
1 steamer large enough to hold the tin

Coarsely chop the pandan leaves (if using). Put the leaves in a saucepan and add the water. Bring to a simmer and cook for 5 minutes. Remove from the heat and allow to infuse. If you are not using pandan leaves, skip this step and pour the water directly into the blender (for a firmer cake, you can even omit the water from the recipe).

Peel the cassava, cut it into small pieces and clean it thoroughly in a large bowl of cold water, then drain.

Pour the coconut milk, strained infused water, cassava, sugar and salt into a blender. Blend until smooth. Pour into the cake tin.

Bring water to a boil in a steamer. Steam the cake for 1 hour, checking the water level from time to time. Allow to cool completely before cutting the cake into even-sized pieces. Roll in the shredded coconut before serving.

Resources

Vegetables & fresh herbs

1. Pea eggplant (makua phuang = 'eggplant clusters'). A variety of eggplant with a bitter taste, often associated with green curries and usually added at the end of cooking. These little eggplants add crunch and a touch of bitterness that complement the flavours of the curry (spicy, creamy, sweet, salty). Sold in the chilled fresh produce section.

2. Thai eggplant (makua). Like the pea eggplant, Thai eggplant has a bitter taste. Cut it into quarters and add it to curries at the end of cooking. Sold in the chilled fresh produce section.

3. Banana leaves (see page 252).

4. King oyster mushroom. This mushroom has a firm texture and a delicate flavour, which is well suited to stir-fries or curries. It can be substituted for meat as its texture is similar to that of chicken.

5. Garlic scapes or **Chinese garlic** (ku chai). Garlic scapes resemble spring onions or chives, but have a subtle garlic flavour. They can be used raw or cooked as an aromatic condiment, and can be replaced by garlic chives or spring onion.

6. Betel leaves or **piper la lot** (*Piper sarmentosum*). Leaves with a spicy and peppery taste. They are mainly used as a fragrant wrap for marinated meat or filled with condiments (as in miang kham).

7. Thai basil. A must-have in Thai cuisine! There are two varieties usually found outside Thailand. Horapa basil is the most common, with a slightly aniseed and refreshing taste, and is used in soups and curries. Holy basil, or krapao, has a stronger taste with spicy and peppery notes and is more commonly used in stir-fried dishes.

8. Water spinach. This aquatic plant with hollow stems is available year round in Thailand. It is very cheap and is a commonly eaten vegetable.

9. Makrut lime or **combava.** Only the zest is used.

10. Cassava. Choose firm and heavy roots without stains. Remove the skin and pink membrane, then rinse thoroughly. The flesh should be very white.

11. Lemongrass. A must-have in Thai cuisine! It is present in all curries, soups, salads and in some marinades. Remove the outer leaves, which can be used to add flavour to curries and soups. For salads, use only the tender centre, finely sliced.

12. Taro. Choose medium or large ones (they have a better texture and are more fragrant) that are firm to the touch with smooth skin.

13. Snake beans. Eaten cooked or raw. They can be replaced by green beans.

14. Baby corn. Cook this so it stays crunchy. Sold in the chilled fresh produce section, it's often imported from Thailand, which means its carbon footprint is high, but the taste of the fresh ones is incomparable to the tinned version.

15. Fingerroot or **krachai** (*Boesenbergia rotunda*). A small tuberous root, with a peppery flavour and citrus and ginger notes. It is sold in the chilled fresh produce section, or you can sometimes find it pickled or frozen in Asian grocers.

16. Bok choy or **pak choy.**

17. Lime leaves or **combava**. A must-have in Thai cuisine! Sold in bags or trays in the fresh or frozen produce sections, the intense fragrance and unique lemony taste of these leaves are typical of Thai dishes.

18. Green peppercorns. Found packaged in the chilled fresh produce section.

19. Galangal. A must-have in Thai cuisine! Its lemony and slightly peppery taste adds freshness to dishes. Sold in bags or trays in the fresh or chilled produce section. It can be cut into slices and frozen.

20. Thai chillies. Thai chillies can be red or green and are sold in the fresh produce section. They are very spicy, so it is better to remove the seeds before adding them to recipes.

21. Aji dulce chillies. Aji dulce chillies have a sweet and fruity flavour. They taste like a chilli but without the heat. They can be found in Asian or Caribbean grocery stores. Not to be confused with the Scotch bonnet chilli, which is very strong. Aji dulce chillies have a more elongated shape, whereas Scotch bonnet chillies are rounder and are named for their resemblance to a Scottish tam o' shanter hat.

22. Gai-lan or **Chinese broccoli.**

Resources — 247

Banana blossom

248 —— Resources

Technique

What is it?
The male, tear-shaped flower that hangs at the end of banana fruit clusters. A banana blossom does not taste like banana at all. It has a subtle and sweet flavour, somewhere between a heart of palm, young coconut and artichoke. It can be eaten as a vegetable or cooked in stews and soups, but is most commonly used raw in salads. Yum hua plee (page 62) is a Thai salad recipe that stars this ingredient. It can also be cut into quarters and served with pad thai (page 146) or with khanom jeen nam ya (page 136), where it is minced and used as a garnish.

Where to buy it?
Outside of Thailand, you can find it wrapped in plastic wrap and in the chilled section of Asian grocery stores.

How to prepare it?
Remove the outer petals if they are damaged. Under each petal you will see a small row of undeveloped bananas. These are bitter so should not be eaten. Thinly slice the core starting from the base (**1**). Soak the slices in lemon or vinegar (**2**) for 5 to 10 minutes. This step is important in order to separate the slices from the small banana buds. Soaking will also minimise oxidation and remove the slight bitter taste. Drain in a colander, separating the slices from the buds and discarding the buds (**3**). Eat soon after preparing.

Resources — 249

Pandan leaves

Technique

What is it?
Pandan is a tropical plant native to Southeast Asia. It has an indescribable floral flavour, a herbal blend reminiscent of almond and coconut. It is often referred to as Asian vanilla, which is why it is frequently used for making desserts and drinks. Its intense green colour also serves as a natural food colouring agent.

Where to buy them?
Pandan leaves can be found in the chilled section of Asian grocery stores. Tinned and frozen juices are also available, but I do not recommend these products as they have no flavour. It is better to use a flavouring essence sold in a bottle, albeit artificial, but at least it captures the taste of pandan.

How to prepare pandan extract?
Clean 120 g (4¼ oz) leaves and cut them into even-sized 1 to 2 cm (½ to ¾ inch) pieces. Add to a blender with 150 ml (generous ½ cup) water and blend. Pour into a cheesecloth and squeeze firmly over a sieve to collect the concentrated juice (**1–2**). Discard any residual leaves. The extract can be kept in the refrigerator for 4 days. After resting overnight in the refrigerator, the water will separate from the chlorophyll, which forms a deposit at the bottom. Gently tip off the water to get an even more fragrant pandan concentrate.

Note
In some traditional restaurants, a small pandan knot is infused into carafes of iced water. The water is subtly fragrant and very refreshing.

Resources — 251

Banana leaves

Banana leaves are used as a natural wrapping for cooking food, while imparting a light flavour to dishes. They can be found in the chilled fresh or frozen produce section of Asian grocery stores.

Preparation

1. Leaves are rarely completely intact. Unfold them gently. First, cut the places where the leaf is torn. Set aside the pieces that are not the correct size; they can be used to reinforce a fold. Store any excess by wrapping in plastic wrap and storing in the freezer. The leaves can easily be thawed and then frozen again.
2. Rinse the leaves thoroughly with water, then wipe dry. Using scissors, remove the rigid central rib that will get in the way when folding and cut out the desired shape.

Tip: If the leaves are brittle and difficult to handle, soak them in boiling water or place them in a hot oven for 1 minute. Both sides can also be quickly passed over the flame of a gas cooker or blowtorch. The heat softens the leaf's fibres.

Resources — 253

Store-bought pastes & sauces

1. Fermented red soy paste. Chinese paste found in jars.
2. Curry paste, Cock brand (massaman, green and red). A must-have. A very practical alternative to homemade pastes. Once opened, these pastes will keep for a year tightly sealed in the refrigerator. Also available in a 50 g (1¾ oz) sachet.
3. Shrimp paste (kapi). A prawn and salt mixture that is left to ferment. The result is a thick dark purple paste. Kapi has an intense smell and flavour that adds depth of taste to seasonings. Once opened, it will keep for a year tightly sealed in the refrigerator. Be sure to choose a paste from Thailand, because products from Indonesia and Malaysia do not taste the same.

4. Preserved radish. Salted and fermented white radish with a crunchy texture. This adds a little extra taste for an authentic pad thai (recipe page 146). It can be replaced with Japanese marinated yellow radish (takuan). Once the bag is opened, it will keep for years in the refrigerator as long as it is well sealed.
5. Salted soy beans. I recommend Yeo's fermented soy beans. Use for Hainan chicken sauce or to stir-fry water spinach.
6. Tamarind paste. A must-have ingredient in Thai cuisine! Be sure to choose a paste from Thailand because products from India do not taste the same.

254 —— Resources

7. Dried shrimp. Sold in the chilled section, choose size XL (2–3 cm/¾–1¼ inches). Soak them for 5 minutes in warm water, or 30 minutes in cold water, before using.

8. Tamarind concentrate, Cook brand. This is practical if you do not have time to soak the paste, but contains preservatives and additives. To make 180 g (6½ oz) homemade tamarind concentrate, dilute 60 g (2¼ oz) crumbled tamarind paste in 200 ml (generous ¾ cup) boiling water. Set aside for 10 minutes. Stir by pressing the paste with the back of a spoon, then strain to collect as much pulp as possible. A thick and concentrated juice will be obtained.

9. Chilli paste (nam prik pao), Thai Dancer brand. A thick paste made from dried shrimp, chillies, garlic, onion and palm sugar. It is an essential ingredient in tom yum soup (recipe page 120). Sold in a jar, it will keep for a year in the refrigerator as long as a layer of oil covers the paste.

10. Palm sugar. A must-have. It comes from the sap of the nipa palm that is boiled until it thickens, then shaped into bricks or cakes. It is a natural sugar, with a low glycaemic index, less sweet than cane sugar. It has a nice amber colour and a slight caramel flavour. Chop it coarsely and heat it with a little water to return it to its liquid form. It can be replaced with raw cane sugar mixed with 1 to 2 tablespoons maple syrup.

11. Sriracha sauce. Created in the town of Sri Racha in the 1930s, this sauce is a mixture of red chillies, garlic, vinegar, sugar and salt. The most famous brand was launched in the 1980s by Huy Fong Foods. I have a preference for the Golden Mountain brand.

12. Fish sauce (nam pla in Thai, nuoc mam in Vietnamese). A must-have in Thai cuisine! It has existed in the region since ancient times. Whether you choose a Thai or Vietnamese sauce, it will not affect the recipe. I like to use Phu Quoc fish sauce as it has a more complex and deeper flavour.

13. Fermented fish sauce (padaek or mam nem in Vietnamese), Pantai brand. This thick sauce is often dark in colour and has an intense smell and a powerful taste (not to be confused with fish sauce: nuoc mam).

14. Oyster sauce. I recommend the brands Lee Kum Kee (Premium or Panda) and Mega Chef (without glutamate, but harder to find).

15. Light soy sauce. Thai or Japanese.

16. Dark soy sauce. Thicker than traditional soy sauce, it is mainly used to add a brown colour to dishes. I recommend Healthy Boy black soy sauce (Thai) or Pearl River Bridge mushroom-flavoured dark soy sauce (Chinese). Thai is sweeter, Chinese is more salty and concentrated (to be used sparingly).

Resources — 255

Basic pantry items

1. Coconut milk. A must-have in Thai cuisine! It is diluted coconut cream or made from the second pressing. It can be found tinned or in long-life packs. Choose one made in Thailand or Indonesia with a good coconut extract content (minimum 60%).

2. Jackfruit in syrup. Jackfruit is the largest fruit in the world and can weigh up to 40 kg (6½ stones). The seeds become yellow when ripe and ready to eat. Its taste is reminiscent of a blend of mango, banana and pineapple. Avoid fresh fruit packaged on trays (they are too green and are not suitable for desserts) as well as frozen fruit (too ripe, they lose their texture after thawing).

3. Palm seeds in syrup (attap). Oval nuts with slightly gelatinous flesh. Not to be confused with toddy palm's seeds. These are two species of palm trees producing different fruits.

4. Water chestnuts. With a soft and crunchy flesh, they are used to add a touch of freshness to meat fillings or to make rubies (dessert). After opening, freeze the rest of the pack in small zip-lock bags.

5. Tapioca pearls.

6. Black glutinous rice. Its colour comes from the natural pigments present in the outer bran of the grains. It has a hazelnut flavour that is characteristic of black rice and goes perfectly with coconut milk. Just like white glutinous rice, it must be soaked before cooking.

7. Rice flour.

8. Shelled mung beans, generally used for making savoury or sweet fillings.

9. Water chestnut starch. A fine powder made from the roots of the water chestnut. It is often used as a thickener because it has a smooth texture with a slightly gelatinous consistency. It is gluten-free and low in calories. Used in making lod chong (recipe page 220).

10. Tapioca starch or **flour.** Made from cassava root and used as a thickener. It imparts the slightly sticky texture found in soups and sauces served in Asian restaurants. It also adds a stretchy consistency to various doughs.

11. Glutinous rice flour. With a higher starch content than rice flour, it has a sticky and elastic texture. It is mainly used in desserts or for some savoury dishes such as the dough for khanom tian (recipe page 42).

256 — Resources

Resources — 257

Noodles

Dried noodles

These include those that are steam-cooked in large sheets and then cut, as well as those that are extruded like spaghetti. The noodles are then dried before being packaged.

Note: They must be soaked before use.

Fresh noodles

Exactly the same as dried noodles, but they were not passed through the dehydrator. They are found in the chilled section, often next to tofu. There are two main types:

Fresh steamed rice noodles (hu tieu, kway teow) are sold either in a block to be cut at home or pre-cut and packaged in large containers. The noodles must be separated before cooking. Heat them in the microwave for a few seconds to make the task easier. These are the noodles used in pad see ew (recipe page 148) and raad na (recipe page 152). **Fresh rice noodles are also sold in vacuum packs** that do not require soaking before use. They have a more elastic texture and break less easily than dried noodles.

Rice vermicelli

Vietnamese rice vermicelli are cooked in a saucepan of boiling water, then drained and rinsed thoroughly to remove the starch. They are drained again and served cold, either by pouring hot soup over them (as in khanom jeen nam ya, recipe page 136), or as a salad (as in sao nam, recipe page 68).

Noodle sizes

At a noodle stand in Thailand, when you order your dish you specify the size of the noodles you would like and if you want them in soup or 'dry'. Dry noodles are seasoned with a mixture of sauces (soy sauce, fish sauce, sugar, chilli etc.). The different sizes are:
· sen lek: thinnest size (2 mm/$\frac{1}{16}$ inch);
· sen gang: medium width (3–4 mm/$\frac{1}{8}$ inch); and
· sen yai: widest (5 mm +/$\frac{1}{4}$ inch +).
Thais are rather fond of thin noodles, especially in soups, because they quickly absorb the flavours of the broth. Wide noodles are reserved for stir-fries, although it is very common to see pad thai made with thin noodles. It's a matter of taste. Stir-fried thin noodles are more moist and sticky, but soak up the sauce better.

1. Fresh rice noodles (ho fun, hu tieu or kway teow, depending on the dialect). These noodles are of Chinese origin and are found in the chilled section.
2. Mung bean vermicelli.
3. Dried rice noodles 1 cm ($\frac{1}{2}$ inch).
4. Dried rice noodles 5 mm ($\frac{1}{4}$ inch).
5. Vietnamese rice vermicelli (bun tuoi).
6. Fresh wheat egg noodles.
7. Triangular rice noodles or rice flake noodles.
8. Rice vermicelli (Wai Wai brand).

Utensils

1. Wok. The golden rule for the wok is to not overfill it. This allows for circulation of hot air around the food, as well as a more even temperature when food comes in contact with the wok. It also makes it easier to mix in circular movements. This is why it is best to cook in batches when a large amount of ingredients needs to be stir-fried. There are two types of wok.
Traditional steel: this is preferred for a gas cooktop. It requires seasoning before use, which gives it a protective layer or natural coating. Once well seasoned, a steel wok will last almost forever.
Non-stick: practical to use (although a little heavy), a non-stick wok is suited to all cooktops but needs to be replaced when its coating ages.

2. Cake tins.

3. Steamer. I prefer steamers with large baskets. Whether they are made of stainless steel or aluminium (be careful with induction cooktops), they are practical because you can bake everything in one go or bake large pieces, like a whole fish or a cake.

4. Chopping board.

5. Papaya grater. See page 46 for use. It can be found in Asian supermarkets. Inexpensive, slimline and easy to use, I always take it with me on holiday.

When I use this grater, I know I will always get a crunchy carrot salad, whereas standard graters either make mush or pieces that are too big. Once you try it, you'll never look back!

6. Knives. A lot of vegetable cutting is required in Thai cuisine. Most of the time, I use a knife with a wide, square blade as a universal knife. It can be replaced by a slicing knife or a Santoku knife (which is a Japanese version).

7. Bamboo basket. This keeps the rice warm and allows good air circulation, which prevents the rice from losing the texture of its grains by becoming too moist.

8. Small stone spice mortar. Allows you to grind small quantities of spices.

9. Large terracotta or hardwood mortar (teak or rosewood). Every home in Thailand has a mortar! It is used to crush and grind all kinds of ingredients: chillies, garlic, herbs, aromatic roots, curry pastes, sauces, papaya salad and more. The mortar is used so often that the aromatics leave their scents and flavours in it. Even when you order a papaya salad without chilli from a street stall, it will be spicy just from the mortar!

Resources — 261

Recipe list

Snacks & starters ●12

Miang Kham	14
Saku Sai Moo	16
Gai Tod Hat Yai	18
Mee Krob	20
Moo Satay	22
Gai Hor Bai Toey	24
Tod Man Pla	26
Thai beers	29
Kuung Tod	30
Khai Luuk Kheuy	32
Po Pia Tod	34
Karipap	38
Khanom Tian	42

Salads & dips ●44

Cutting papaya & mango	46
Som Tum	48
Nam Tok	50
Yum Talay	52
Larb Gai	54
Yum Som-O	56
Yum Woon Sen	58
Yum Makeua Yao	60
Yum Hua Plee	62
Yum Phed	64
Sao Nam	68
Yum Mama	70
Pla Rad Prik	72
Salmon Larb dip	74
Larb dip	76
Nam Prik Kapi	78
Chiang Mai dips	80
Dips we make at home	82

Curries ●84

Curry pastes	86
Gaeng Kiew Wan	88
Gaeng Khiao Wan Kuung Mamuang	90
Gaeng Ped Moo Nor Mai	92
Gaeng Ped Phed Sapparot	94
Gaeng Pha	96
Gaeng Massaman Nua	98
Gaeng Hung Lay	100
Panang Nua	104
Choo Chee Pla	106
Gaeng Na Nao	108
Gaeng Na Ron	110
Khao Niaow	112
Khao San	114

Soups ●116

Basic broth	118
Tom Yum Kuung	120
Tom Kha Gai	122
Gaeng Som	124
Gaeng Liang	126
Yen Ta Fo	128
Guay Jab	130
Bami Phet	132
Mee Kati	134
Khanom Jeen Nam Ya	136
Khao Soi	138
Sukiyaki	140

Stir-fries

144

Pad Thai	146
Pad See Ew	148
Pad Kee Mao	150
Raad Na	152
Pad Woon Sen Kai	154
Pad Prik King	156
Pad Horapa Moo	158
Pad Phed	160
Gai Pad King	162
Gai Pad Med Mamuang	164
Pad Priew Wan	166
Khao Pad Kai	168
Khao Pad Gai Tom Yum	170
Khao Pad Sapparot	172
Pad Pak Boong Fai Daeng	174
Pad Het Prik Thai Sod	176
Pad Pak Ruam Mit	178

Meat & seafood

180

Aeb Pla	182
Pla Neung Manao	184
Mok Pla folding	186
Mok Pla	188
Pla Tod Yam Mamuang	190
Pla Sam Rot	192
Pla Muk Yad Sai	196
Ob Woon Sen	198
Kha Moo Palo	200
Khao Man Gai	202
Crying tiger	204
Gai Yang	206
Moo Wan	208
Sai Oua	210
Mok Gai	212

Drinks & desserts

214

Nam Dao Huu	216
Gafae Yen	218
Lod Chong Ruam Mit	220
Kluay Buat Chee	222
Khao Taen	224
Khanom Mo Kaeng	226
Sangkaya Fak Thong	228
Khao Tom Mut	230
Itim Kathi	232
Woon Phon Lamai	234
Khanom Chan	236
Khao Niao Mamuang	238
Khao Niao Dam	240
Khanom Man Sampalang	242

Resources

244

Vegetables & fresh herbs	246
Banana blossom	248
Pandan leaves	250
Banana leaves	252
Store-bought pastes & sauces	254
Basic pantry items	256
Noodles	258
Utensils	260
Recipe list	262
Index	264

Index by ingredients

Bamboo shoots
Gaeng Ped Moo
Nor Mai **92**

Banana & plantain
Kluay Buat Chee **222**
Khao Tom Mut **230**

Banana blossom
Yum Hua Plee **62**

Banana leaves
Khanom Tian **42**
Aeb Pla **182**
Mok Pla **188**
Mok Gai **212**
Khao Tom Mut **230**

Basic broth
Tom Yum Kuung **120**
Gaeng Som **124**
Gaeng Liang **126**
Yen Ta Fo **128**
Guay Jab **130**
Bami Phet **132**
Sukiyaki **140**
Pla Neung Manao **184**
Ob Woon Sen **198**

Beef
Nam Tok **50**
Larb dip **76**
Gaeng Massaman
Nua **98**
Panang Nua **104**
Sukiyaki **140**
Pad See Ew **148**
Crying tiger **204**

Berries
Woon Phon Lamai **234**

Betel
Miang Kham **14**

Cabbage
Po Pia Tod **34**
Nam Prik Kapi **78**
Gaeng Som **124**
Raad Na **152**
Mok Pla **188**

Capsicum (pepper)
Nam Prik Noom **80**
Gaeng Kiew Wan **88**
Panang Nua **104**
Gaeng Na Ron **110**
Pad Phed **160**
Gai Pad Med Mamuang **164**

Cassava
Khanom Man
Sampalang **242**

Chicken
Gai Tod Hat Yai **18**
Gai Hor Bai Toey **24**
Karipap **38**
Larb Gai **54**
Yum Hua Plee **62**
Yum Mama **70**
Gaeng Kiew Wan **88**
Gaeng Pha **96**
Basic broth **118**
Tom Kha Gai **122**
Khao Soi **138**
Sukiyaki **140**
Gai Pad King **162**
Gai Pad Med Mamuang **164**
Khao Pad Gai Tom
Yum **170**
Khao Man Gai **202**
Gai Yang **206**
Mok Gai **212**

Chilli
Almost all recipes!

Chilli paste (nam prik pao)
Yum Talay **52**
Yum Hua Plee **62**
Tom Yum Kuung **120**
Gai Pad Med Mamuang **164**
Khao Pad Gai Tom Yum **170**

Chinese broccoli (gai-lan)
Pad See Ew **148**

Choko (chayote)
Gaeng Na Nao **108**
Gaeng Liang **126**

Coconut milk & cream
Moo Satay **22**
Yum Hua Plee **62**
Sao Nam **68**
Gaeng Kiew Wan **88**
Gaeng Khiao Wan Kuung
Mamuang **90**
Gaeng Ped Moo Nor Mai **92**
Gaeng Ped Phed
Sapparot **94**
Gaeng Massaman Nua **98**
Panang Nua **104**
Choo Chee Pla **106**
Gaeng Na Nao **108**
Gaeng Na Ron **110**
Tom Kha Gai **122**
Mee Kati **134**
Khanom Jeen Nam Ya **136**
Khao Soi **138**
Pad Phed **160**
Mok Pla **188**
Lod Chong Ruam Mit **220**
Kluay Buat Chee **222**
Khanom Mo Kaeng **226**
Sangkaya Fak Thong **228**
Khao Tom Mut **230**
Itim Kathi **232**
Woon Phon Lamai **234**
Khanom Chan **236**
Khao Niao Mamuang **238**
Khanom Man
Sampalang **242**

Coffee
Gafae Yen **218**

Condensed milk
Gafae Yen **218**

Cucumber
Moo Satay **22**
Tod Man Pla **26**

Curry pastes
— green
Gaeng Kiew Wan **88**
Gaeng Khiao Wan Kuung
Mamuang **90**
— massaman
Karipap **38**
Gaeng Massaman Nua **98**
Gaeng Na Nao **108**

264 — Index

— red

Moo Satay **22**
Tod Man Pla **26**
Kuung Tod **30**
Gaeng Ped Moo
 Nor Mai **92**
Gaeng Ped Phed
 Sapparot **94**
Gaeng Pha **96**
Panang Nua **104**
Choo Chee Pla **106**
Mee Kati **134**
Khanom Jeen Nam
 Ya **136**
Khao Soi **138**
Pad Prik King **156**
Mok Pla **188**
Sai Oua **210**

Daikon

Gaeng Som **124**

Duck

Yum Phed **64**
Gaeng Ped Phed
 Sapparot **94**
Bami Phet **132**
Pad Phed **160**

Eggplant (aubergine)

Yum Makeua Yao **60**
Gaeng Na Ron **110**

Eggs

Khai Luuk Kheuy **32**
Guay Jab **130**
Khao Pad Kai **168**
Kha Moo Palo **200**

Fermented fish sauce (padaek)

Som Tum **48**
Larb dip **76**
Nam Prik Makua
 Thet **82**

Fermented salted soy beans

Mee Kati **134**
Khao Man Gai **202**

Fermented shrimp paste (kapi)

Miang Kham **14**
Nam Prik Kapi **78**
Nam Prik Ong **80**
Curry pastes **86**
Gaeng Hung Lay **100**
Gaeng Som **124**
Gaeng Liang **126**

Fingerroot (krachai)

Gaeng Pha **96**
Gaeng Som **124**
Gaeng Liang **126**
Khanom Jeen Nam Ya **136**

Fish & Seafood

Tod Man Pla **26**
Yum Talay **52**
Pla Rad Prik **72**
Salmon Larb dip **74**
Nam Prik Kapi **78**
Choo Chee Pla **106**
Gaeng Som **124**
Khanom Jeen Nam Ya **136**
Sukiyaki **140**
Aeb Pla **182**
Pla Neung Manao **184**
Mok Pla **188**
Pla Tod Yam Mamuang **190**
Pla Sam Rot **192**
Pla Muk Yad Sai **196**

Galangal

Miang Kham **14**
Salmon Larb dip **74**
Larb dip **76**
Curry pastes **86**
Gaeng Kiew Wan **88**
Gaeng Ped Moo Nor Mai **92**
Gaeng Hung Lay **100**
Tom Yum Kuung **120**
Tom Kha Gai **122**
Bami Phet **132**
Khanom Jeen Nam Ya **136**
Khao Soi **138**
Khao Pad Gai Tom Yum **170**
Mok Gai **212**

Ginger

Miang Kham **14**
Sao Nam **68**

Gaeng Hung Lay **100**
Guay Jab **130**
Gai Pad King **162**
Khao Pad Sapparot **172**
Ob Woon Sen **198**
Kha Moo Palo **200**
Khao Man Gai **202**
Gai Yang **206**
Moo Wan **208**

Glutinous rice flour

Khanom Tian **42**

Jackfruit

Lod Chong Ruam
 Mit **220**

Lemongrass

Nam Tok **50**
Yum Talay **52**
Pla Rad Prik **72**
Salmon Larb dip **74**
Larb dip **76**
Nam Prik Ong **80**
Curry pastes **86**
Gaeng Kiew Wan **88**
Gaeng Ped Moo Nor
 Mai **92**
Gaeng Ped Phed
 Sapparot **94**
Gaeng Pha **96**
Gaeng Massaman Nua **98**
Gaeng Hung Lay **100**
Panang Nua **104**
Tom Yum Kuung **120**
Mee Kati **134**
Khanom Jeen Nam Ya **136**
Khao Soi **138**
Khao Pad Gai Tom Yum **170**
Aeb Pla **182**
Pla Neung Manao **184**
Gai Yang **206**
Sai Oua **210**
Mok Gai **212**

Lime

Tod Man Pla **26**
Salmon Larb dip **74**
Curry pastes **86**
Gaeng Kiew Wan **88**
Gaeng Ped Moo Nor
 Mai **92**

Index —— 265

Gaeng Ped Phed
Sapparot **94**
Gaeng Pha **96**
Panang Nua **104**
Choo Chee Pla **106**
Tom Yum Kuung **120**
Tom Kha Gai **122**
Khanom Jeen Nam Ya **136**
Pad Prik King **156**
Pad Phed **160**
Khao Pad Gai Tom Yum **170**
Aeb Pla **182**
Mok Pla **188**
Sai Oua **210**

Lychee
Woon Phon Lamai **234**

Mango
Gaeng Khiao Wan Kuung
Mamuang **90**
Pla Tod Yam Mamuang **190**
Khao Niao Mamuang **238**

Mung beans & bean sprouts
Khanom Tian **42**
Bami Phet **132**
Mee Kati **134**
Pad Thai **146**
Pad Woon Sen Kai **154**

Mushrooms
— black
Po Pia Tod **34**
Gai Pad King **162**
— button
Nam Prik Hed **82**
— king oyster
Pad Het Prik Thai Sod **176**
— shiitake
Sukiyaki **140**
Raad Na **152**
Pad Pak Ruam Mit **178**
— shimeji
Gaeng Na Nao **108**
Sukiyaki **140**

Noodles
— instant
Yum Mama **70**

— rice
Mee Kati **134**
Pad Thai **146**
Pad See Ew **148**
Pad Kee Mao **150**
Raad Na **152**
— wheat
Bami Phet **132**
Khao Soi **138**

Okra
Nam Prik Kapi **78**

Palm fruit
Lod Chong Ruam Mit **220**

Pandan
Gai Hor Bai Toey **24**
Lod Chong Ruam Mit **220**
Sangkaya Fak Thong **228**
Khanom Chan **236**
Khanom Man
Sampalang **242**

Papaya
Som Tum **48**

Peanuts
Miang Kham **14**
Moo Satay **22**
Gaeng Massaman
Nua **98**
Gaeng Na Nao **108**

Pineapple
Sao Nam **68**
Gaeng Ped Phed
Sapparot **94**
Pad Priew Wan **166**
Khao Pad Sapparot **172**

Pomelo
Yum Som-O **56**

Pork
Saku Sai Moo **16**
Moo Satay **22**
Khai Luuk Kheuy **32**
Po Pia Tod **34**
Khanom Tian **42**
Yum Woon Sen **58**

Yum Mama **70**
Nam Prik Ong **80**
Gaeng Ped Moo Nor
Mai **92**
Gaeng Hung Lay **100**
Basic broth **118**
Guay Jab **130**
Mee Kati **134**
Pad Thai **146**
Raad Na **152**
Pad Prik King **156**
Pad Horapa Moo **158**
Pla Muk Yad Sai **196**
Kha Moo Palo **200**
Moo Wan **208**
Sai Oua **210**

Prawns & shrimp
— dried
Miang Kham **14**
Nam Prik Kapi **78**
Gaeng Liang **126**
Pad Thai **146**
— fresh or frozen
Kuung Tod **30**
Po Pia Tod **34**
Yum Talay **52**
Yum Som-O **56**
Yum Woon Sen **58**
Sao Nam **68**
Gaeng Khiao Wan Kuung
Mamuang **90**
Tom Yum Kuung **120**
Gaeng Liang **126**
Yen Ta Fo **128**
Sukiyaki **140**
Pad Thai **146**
Pad Kee Mao **150**
Khao Pad Sapparot **172**
Ob Woon Sen **198**

Rice
— glutinous
Larb Gai **54**
Yum Phed **64**
Larb dip **76**
Khao Niaow **112**
Crying tiger **204**
Khao Taen **224**
Khao Tom Mut **230**
Khao Niao Mamuang **238**
Khao Niao Dam **240**

— jasmine
Khao Man Gai **202**
Crying tiger **204**
— Thai
Khao San **114**
Khao Pad Kai **168**
Khao Pad Gai Tom Yum **170**
Khao Pad Sapparot **172**

Rice flake noodles
Guay Jab **130**

Rice flakes
Kuung Tod **30**

Salted Chinese radish
Saku Sai Moo **16**
Pad Thai **146**

Sichuan pepper
Kha Moo Palo **200**

Snake beans
Tod Man Pla **26**
Som Tum **48**

Snow peas (mange tout)
Gaeng Kiew Wan **88**

Spring roll wrappers
Po Pia Tod **34**

Squash
Nam Prik Kapi **78**
Gaeng Na Nao **108**
Gaeng Liang **126**
Sangkaya Fak Thong **228**

Tamarind
Miang Kham **14**
Mee Krob **20**
Khai Luuk Kheuy **32**
Yum Hua Plee **62**
Yum Phed **64**
Gaeng Hung Lay **100**
Gaeng Som **124**
Sukiyaki **140**
Pad Thai **146**
Pad Phed **160**
Pla Sam Rot **192**
Crying tiger **204**

Tapioca
Saku Sai Moo **16**
Kluay Buat Chee **222**

Taro
Po Pia Tod **34**
Khanom Mo Kaeng **226**

Thai basil
Salmon Larb dip **74**
Curry pastes **86**
Gaeng Kiew Wan **88**
Gaeng Khiao Wan Kuung
   Mamuang **90**
Gaeng Ped Phed
   Sapparot **94**
Gaeng Na Ron **110**
Gaeng Liang **126**
Pad Kee Mao **150**
Pad Horapa Moo **158**
Pad Phed **160**
Mok Pla **188**

**Thai eggplant
(aubergine)**
Nam Prik Kapi **78**
Gaeng Pha **96**

**Thai pea eggplant
(aubergine)**
Gaeng Pha **96**

Tofu
Gaeng Na Nao **108**
Yen Ta Fo **128**
Guay Jab **130**
Sukiyaki **140**
Pad Priew Wan **166**

Tomato & cherry tomato
Nam Prik Ong **80**
Nam Prik Makua Thet **82**

Vermicelli
— bean thread
Po Pia Tod **34**
Yum Woon Sen **58**
Sukiyaki **140**
Pad Woon Sen Kai **154**
Pla Muk Yad Sai **196**
Ob Woon Sen **198**

— rice
Mee Krob **20**
Sao Nam **68**
Yen Ta Fo **128**
Khanom Jeen Nam Ya **136**

Water chestnuts
Po Pia Tod **34**
Lod Chong Ruam Mit **220**

Water spinach
Nam Prik Kapi **78**
Gaeng Som **124**
Yen Ta Fo **128**
Sukiyaki **140**
Pad Pak Boong Fai
   Daeng **174**

Yellow soy beans
Nam Dao Huu **216**

Zucchini (courgette)
Gaeng Kiew Wan **88**
Gaeng Na Ron **110**

Index — 267

Acknowledgements

Thank you to my editors Audrey & Christine, who entrusted me with this magnificent project, which was initially due to be written in Bangkok before Covid.
Thank you to Akiko for your gentleness and for all the lovely moments spent together during our unforgettable Japanese road trip.
Thank you Élise for your efficiency and all the stories we shared.
Thank you Élodie for your flawless taste.
Thank you Lola, Mila, Sienna and Eythan, you are all so beautiful!
To my parents, my brother and my aunts.
To my sisters K. & V.
To JY.

Published in 2024 by Murdoch Books, an imprint of Allen & Unwin
First published in 2023 by Hachette Livre (Marabout)

Murdoch Books Australia
Cammeraygal Country
83 Alexander Street
Crows Nest NSW 2065
Phone: +61 (0)2 8425 0100
murdochbooks.com.au
info@murdochbooks.com.au

Murdoch Books UK
Ormond House
26–27 Boswell Street
London WC1N 3JZ
Phone: +44 (0) 20 8785 5995
murdochbooks.co.uk
info@murdochbooks.co.uk

For corporate orders and custom publishing, contact our business development team at salesenquiries@murdochbooks.com.au

Photography: Akiko Ida
Styling: Élodie Rambaud
Graphic design: Pierre Jeanneau
Layout: Francine Thierry
Proofreading: Élise Peylet and Irène Colas

Publisher: Justin Wolfers
Translator: Nicola Thayil
English-language editor: Kay Halsey
English-language designer and cover designer: Sarah McCoy
Production director: Lou Playfair

Text, photography and internal design © Hachette Livre (Marabout) 2023
The moral right of the author has been asserted.
Cover design © Murdoch Books 2024

Murdoch Books acknowledges the Traditional Owners of the Country on which we live and work. We pay our respects to all Aboriginal and Torres Strait Islander Elders, past and present.

All rights reserved. No part of this publication may be reproduced, stored in a retrieval system or transmitted in any form or by any means, electronic, mechanical, photocopying, recording or otherwise, without the prior written permission of the publisher.

ISBN 978 1 76150 019 0

 A catalogue record for this book is available from the National Library of Australia

A catalogue record for this book is available from the British Library

Printed by 1010 Printing International Limited, China

IMPORTANT: Those who might be at risk from the effects of salmonella poisoning (the elderly, pregnant women, young children and those suffering from immune deficiency diseases) should consult their doctor with any concerns about eating raw eggs. Please ensure that all seafood and beef to be eaten raw or lightly cooked are very fresh and of the highest quality.

TABLESPOON MEASURES: We have used 15 ml (3 teaspoon) tablespoon measures.

10 9 8 7 6 5 4 3 2 1